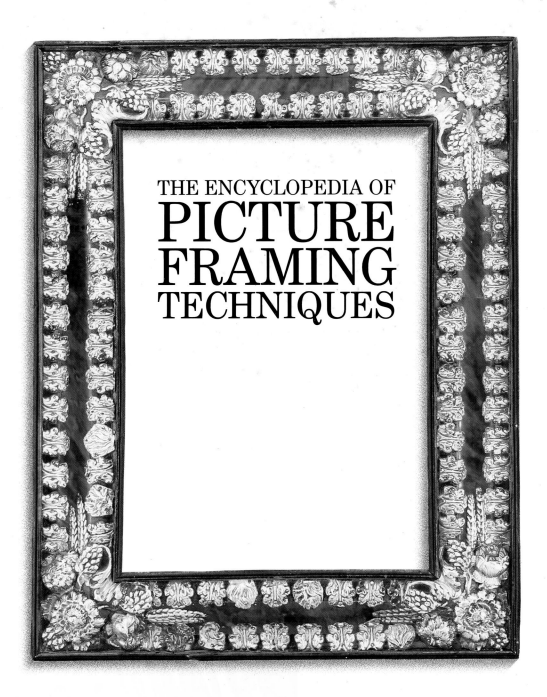

THE ENCYCLOPEDIA OF
PICTURE
FRAMING
TECHNIQUES

This pedimented frame with a marble finish (above) is a modern version of a traditional type. An attractive frame (right) with a lapis lazuli finish. Both pieces were made by Robert Cunning.

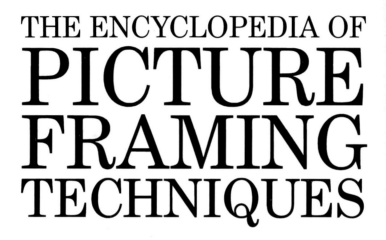

THE ENCYCLOPEDIA OF
PICTURE
FRAMING
TECHNIQUES

ROBERT CUNNING

RUNNING PRESS
PHILADELPHIA, PENNSYLVANIA

A QUARTO BOOK

ISBN 1-56138-208-6

Library of Congress Cataloging-in-Publication
Number 92-50792

This book was designed and produced by
Quarto Publishing plc
The Old Brewery
6 Blundell Street
London N7 9BH

Senior Editor Hazel Harrison
Art Editor Penny Cobb
Designer Terry Jeavons
Photographers Paul Forrester, Ian Howes and Chas Wilder
Picture Researcher Amanda Little
Diagrams Ed Stuart
Art Director Moira Clinch
Publishing Director Janet Slingsby

Typeset in Tunbridge Wells by En to En
Manufactured by Eray Scan, Singapore
Printed in Hong Kong by Leefung Asco. Printers Ltd

This book may be ordered by mail from the
publisher. Please include $2.50 for postage
and handling. *But try your bookstore first!*

Running Press Book Publishers
125 South Twenty-second Street
Philadelphia, Pennsylvania 19103

A delicate paint finish with subtle
touches of gold on the ornament and
inner edge complements the gentle
colors of the floral print. The frame
was made by Patrick Ireland.

CONTENTS

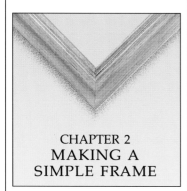
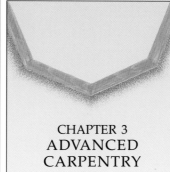

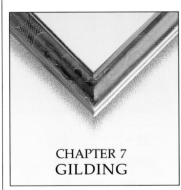

CHAPTER 7
GILDING

CHAPTER 8
**RESTORATION
AND REPAIR**

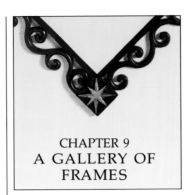

CHAPTER 9
**A GALLERY OF
FRAMES**

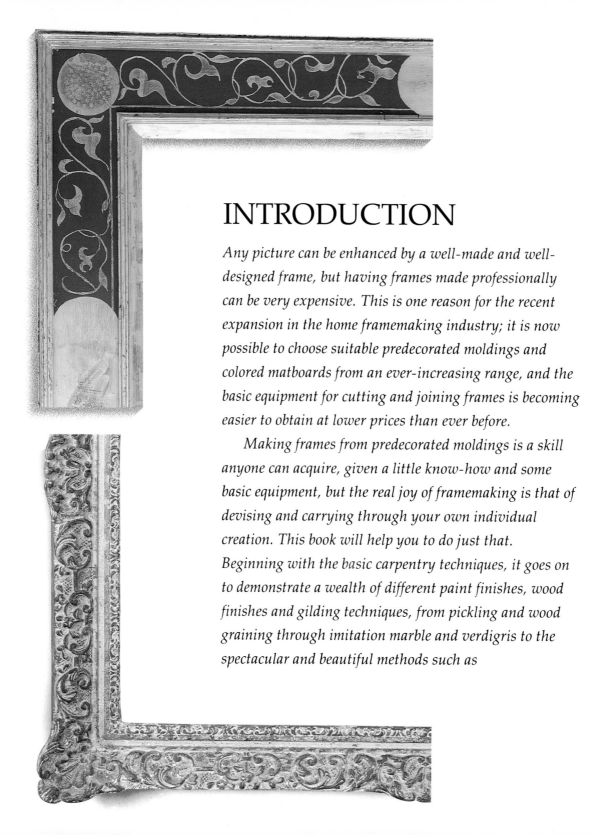

INTRODUCTION

Any picture can be enhanced by a well-made and well-designed frame, but having frames made professionally can be very expensive. This is one reason for the recent expansion in the home framemaking industry; it is now possible to choose suitable predecorated moldings and colored matboards from an ever-increasing range, and the basic equipment for cutting and joining frames is becoming easier to obtain at lower prices than ever before.

Making frames from predecorated moldings is a skill anyone can acquire, given a little know-how and some basic equipment, but the real joy of framemaking is that of devising and carrying through your own individual creation. This book will help you to do just that. Beginning with the basic carpentry techniques, it goes on to demonstrate a wealth of different paint finishes, wood finishes and gilding techniques, from pickling and wood graining through imitation marble and verdigris to the spectacular and beautiful methods such as

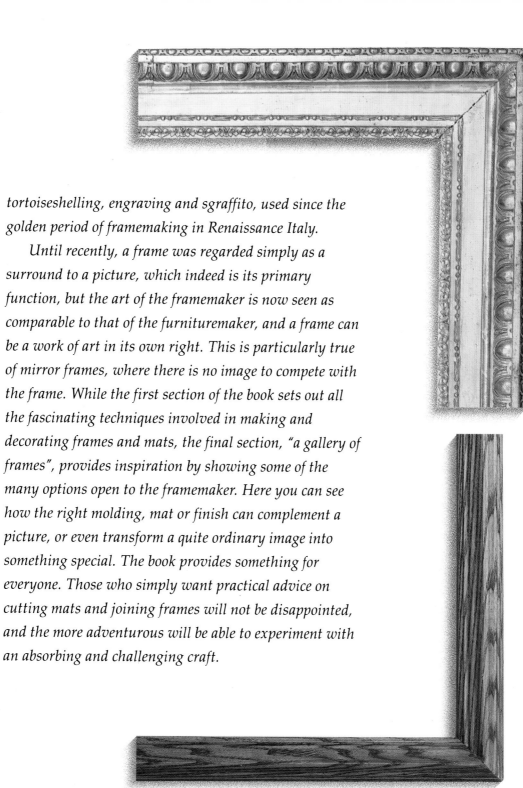

tortoiseshelling, engraving and sgraffito, used since the golden period of framemaking in Renaissance Italy.

Until recently, a frame was regarded simply as a surround to a picture, which indeed is its primary function, but the art of the framemaker is now seen as comparable to that of the furnituremaker, and a frame can be a work of art in its own right. This is particularly true of mirror frames, where there is no image to compete with the frame. While the first section of the book sets out all the fascinating techniques involved in making and decorating frames and mats, the final section, "a gallery of frames", provides inspiration by showing some of the many options open to the framemaker. Here you can see how the right molding, mat or finish can complement a picture, or even transform a quite ordinary image into something special. The book provides something for everyone. Those who simply want practical advice on cutting mats and joining frames will not be disappointed, and the more adventurous will be able to experiment with an absorbing and challenging craft.

CHAPTER 1

MATERIALS AND EQUIPMENT

Few people have large, well-equipped workshops at their disposal; the majority of us have to be satisfied with a small space and a vice or saw attached to the kitchen table. Unless you are planning to make large frames, however, this is usually adequate for the carpentry involved, and frames can be placed on the floor for gluing.

You do not need a great deal of expensive equipment at the outset; you can begin with a small range of hand tools and acquire more sophisticated items as the need arises. The expansion in the do-it-yourself industry has forced manufacturers to become more and more competitive, which has resulted in a wide variety of tools becoming accessible to the amateur enthusiast.

The tools that the professional framemakers use, namely foot-operated guillotine cutters (Morso cutters) and underpinning machines for joining the frame together, have been designed for speed and yield perfect frames within minutes. However, they are both large and expensive, and are not relevant for most home-based framemakers.

SAWS AND CUTTERS

The Morso cutter is probably the machine most widely used by professional framemakers. It is a very well-designed machine and has been in existence for over forty years with very little modification. It does take up a large amount of space, but there are now some smaller versions of the same basic design which are hand-operated and can be clamped onto a small table.

The most essential tool for the home-based framemaker is a good miter saw which is mounted onto a metal base and held in place by two steel columns. There are now many makes available, and they are very reasonably priced. They have largely replaced the traditional wood or metal miter boxes used with a tenon saw. The wooden boxes tend to erode at the edges with use and consequently give inaccurate cuts. The metal ones are better, and when used with a good-quality saw yield accurate results, but they are more difficult to use than miter saws and so have declined in popularity.

Morso cutter
This has two blades mounted on a moving block. It is operated by foot and cuts two miters at the same time.

Trimmer
The trimmer is useful if you are cutting molding with a saw. It is used to slice off small pieces of wood so that the opposite sides of the frame are equal.

Underpinner
1 When pre-decorated moldings are used, the conventional method of joining frames by nailing is tiresome, as the nail holes have to be filled with a matching-colored filler. Underpinning machines dispense with the need for nailing. They fire staples into the frame from the back without leaving any mark on the sides.

2 Gluing and underpinning are done as part of the same process, with the frame in place on a flat desk. The underpinner shown here is a large professional type, but small hand-operated models are now being developed for the do-it-yourself market.

Miter saw

The miter saw is the most important tool for the home-based framemaker. Accurate miter cuts can be made easily, and most miter saws have a built-in protractor so that the angle can be changed for cutting octagons and so on. Most also have a metal arm attached, enabling you to cut a second piece of molding exactly the same size as the first without measuring.

HAND TOOLS

After you have cut the frame it must be glued, and the miter joints held firmly with some form of a clamp.

To help you complete the frame, it is useful to have a few hand tools. A hand or electric drill is essential, particularly for hardwoods. It is almost impossible to nail into a hardwood frame without first drilling a hole. For softwood frames, an awl is usually adequate to make a pilot hole for the nail to sit in before it is driven in by the hammer. These come in a variety of sizes and types, but are basically spikes with wooden handles.

There are many types of pliers, and it is useful, though not essential, to have a selection. The needle-nose type is good for extracting bent and broken nails, and snub-nosed engineering or electrical pliers are for nail straightening and cutting.

A tack hammer, sometimes called a flat-sided hammer, is essential for nailing the sides of the frame, as is a nail set for driving the nail below the surface of the wood. This hole is then filled, sanded, and decorated to match the finish of the frame. Nail sets come in many shapes and sizes, but one general-purpose nail set is all that you need. Those with recessed heads are the most useful type.

The glue most commonly used by framemakers is the quick setting PVA (polyvinyl acetate) type (also known as white or yellow glue). Because of its strength and quick-bonding quality, it has largely replaced the traditional animal glues that need to be mixed and heated. There are many other types of strong glue, such as epoxy resins and casein glues, which are also suitable for joints. All glue deteriorates in time, as can be seen on old frames where there are gaps or movement in the joints. For this reason, it is very important to use nails or other supports as well.

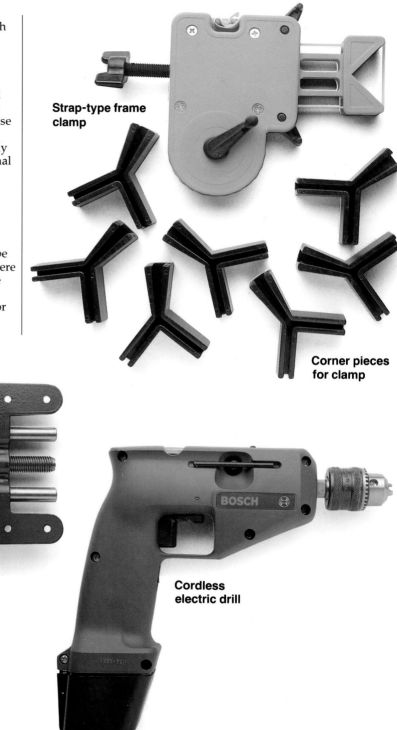

Strap-type frame clamp

Corner pieces for clamp

Vice

Cordless electric drill

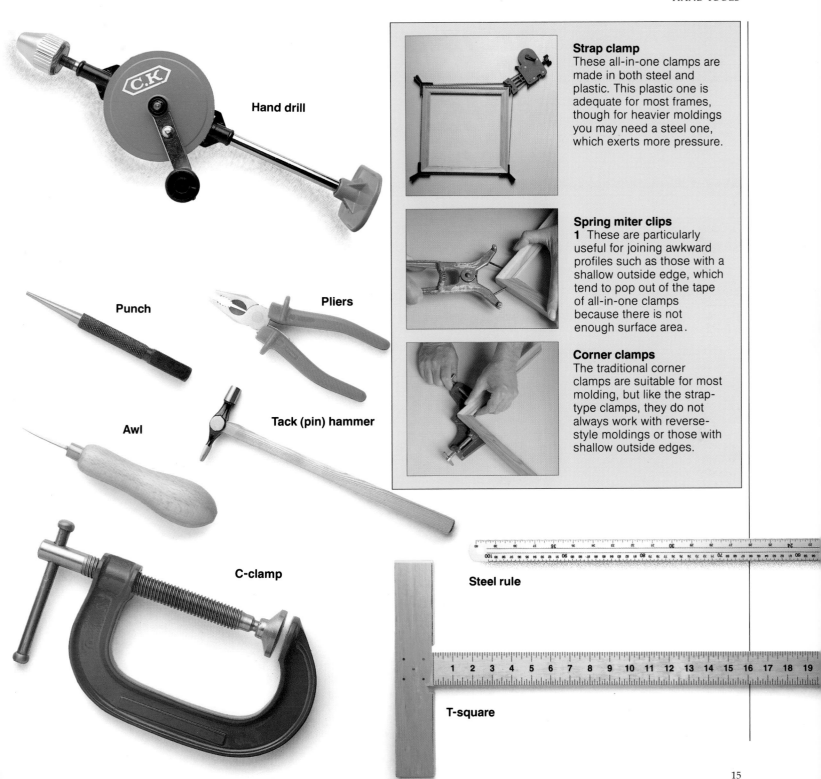

Hand drill

Punch

Pliers

Awl

Tack (pin) hammer

C-clamp

Steel rule

T-square

Strap clamp
These all-in-one clamps are made in both steel and plastic. This plastic one is adequate for most frames, though for heavier moldings you may need a steel one, which exerts more pressure.

Spring miter clips
1 These are particularly useful for joining awkward profiles such as those with a shallow outside edge, which tend to pop out of the tape of all-in-one clamps because there is not enough surface area.

Corner clamps
The traditional corner clamps are suitable for most molding, but like the strap-type clamps, they do not always work with reverse-style moldings or those with shallow outside edges.

MAT CUTTERS

An entire industry has developed around the cutting of beveled edges for the windows of mats.*

Traditionally, this job was done by hand using a sharp knife and a steel straight edge, but it takes practice and considerable skill to cut bevels in this way. The devices now available range from the elaborate bench cutting machines used by professionals to a variety of hand-held cutters.

The American-made Dexter hand-held cutter, which has been in existence for many years, is versatile and well-suited to the beginner. It is heavy enough to cut through the matboard in one push and can also be used to cut ovals and circles.

The Logan cutter gives a generous bevel and will also cut through in one pass. At the present time, it is probably the most sophisticated hand-held cutter available.

The Olfa matcutter is inexpensive and easy to use. The plexiglass base allows you to see the line as you cut, but the lack of weight means that you have to repeat the cut two or three times.

The Maped cutter comes closest to the professional bench cutters. It has a cutter mounted onto a ruler that is used for measuring the window as well as for holding the cutter in place.

Each year, different designs appear. They all need a little practice, but in time will yield good results.

✱FURTHER INFORMATION

Cutting the mat   page 24

▲ This simple cutter, a Cushway, has the same action as the Dexter cutter and uses the same blades. The blades can be mounted at either end, so this is a useful cutter for left-handed people.

▲ The Olfa cutter has a plexiglass base, which allows you to see the line as you cut the bevel. The triangular blades are designed to cut through the board in two or three passes.

▼ This is an adaptation of a small Logan cutter, with a ruler that allows you to cut without drawing lines first.

▼ The Maped cutter works on the same principle as the larger bench cutters and also comes with a vertical cutter for straight lines.

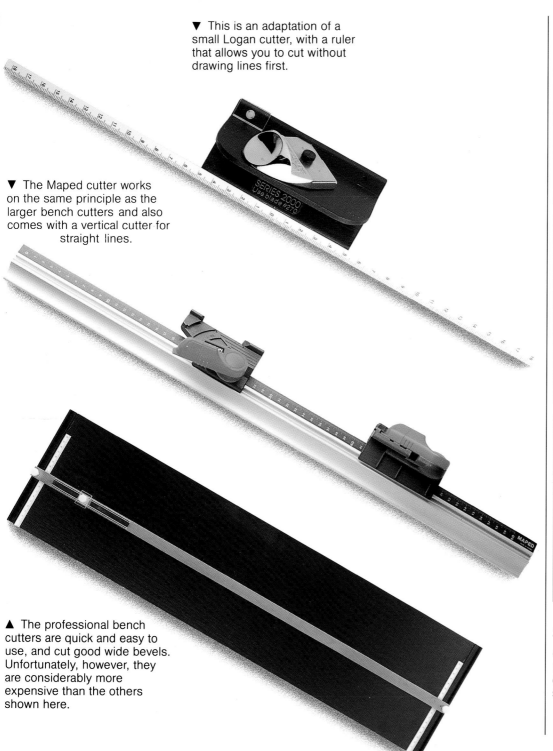

▲ The professional bench cutters are quick and easy to use, and cut good wide bevels. Unfortunately, however, they are considerably more expensive than the others shown here.

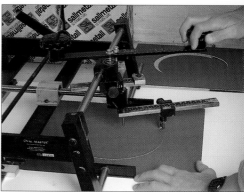

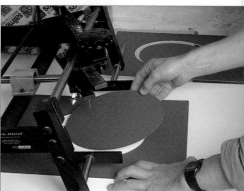

▲ **Oval and circle cutter**
This professional circle and oval cutter has adjustable measuring arms so that different dimensions and shapes can be cut.

MOLDING SHAPES

There are many different types of frame profiles with widths varying from a narrow strip to several inches, but they can be divided into a few main categories.

The swept frame has a high outside edge that sweeps down in a curve to the sight edge. These have been used in the past as foundations for elaborate molded decoration, but they can be used in a plainer manner as a natural wood finished frame and are perennially popular.

The opposite shape to the swept frame is the reverse profile. This has the highest part of the molding near the picture and has the effect of thrusting the picture forward. This type of shape has been known since the 16th century and is still popular and widely used today.

The border frame or cassetta* type combines a flat border within the profile. These borders lend themselves to many styles of decoration, or for more contemporary pictures, can be left plain.

▶ The three moldings at the top are all different variations of the reverse style, with shallow back edges. The middle three are swept moldings, while those at the bottom have flat sections. The latter type is useful for veneering, as wood veneers cannot be applied over intricate shapes or sharp curves.

REVERSE MOLDINGS

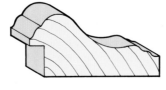

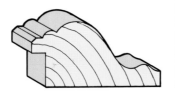

FLAT MOLDINGS

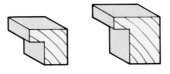

SWEPT MOLDINGS

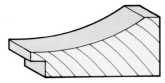
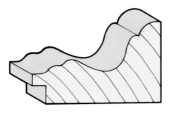
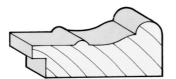

CASSETTA-STYLE MOLDING

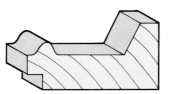

THE PARTS OF THE FRAME

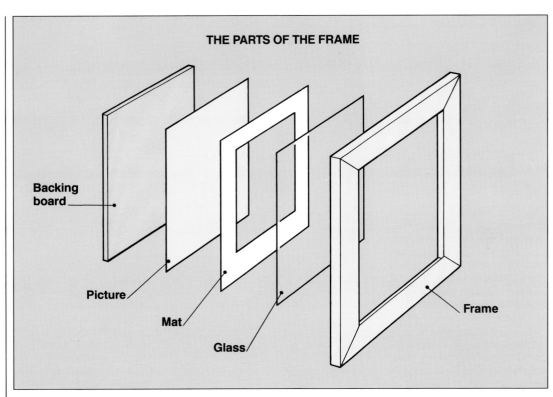

Backing board

Picture

Mat

Glass

Frame

CUSHION MOLDINGS

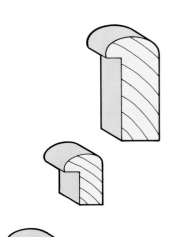

THE PARTS OF THE MOLDING

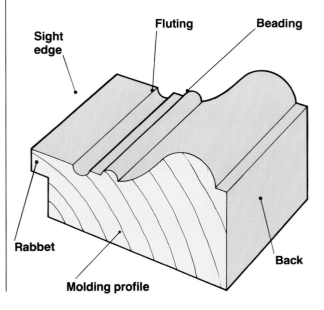

Sight edge

Fluting

Beading

Rabbet

Molding profile

Back

19

DECORATED MOLDINGS

The industry in predecorated moldings has greatly expanded in recent years and tends to follow the fashion of interior designs in interior decoration, fabrics, and furniture. It is only possible to include a few examples of the vast choice available.

Care must be taken when using predecorated moldings, as many have a high gloss or fragile finish which can easily be damaged in the cutting and nailing process.

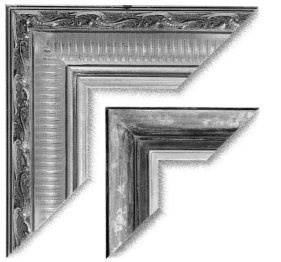

The choice of pre-decorated moldings is constantly increasing, so it is worth looking around to find out what different suppliers can offer. Moldings like these, however, some of which have been designed by a leading framemaking business for their own use, are very expensive, and you may find it ultimately more satisfying – as well as less costly – to decorate your own frames.

▲ This line of stained and veneered wood moldings with gilt sight edges shows the popular colors and shapes of natural-wood frames.

▶ Pickled, veneered, stained, and ebonized natural wood finishes, as well as more richly colored and gilded finishes, are now available as pre-decorated moldings. Traditional shapes and colors as well as contemporary designs are included in most manufacturers' catalogues.

▲ Soft pastel colors have been lightly washed onto the moldings so that the natural grain of the wood is still visible. Gold-foil sight edges add a touch of contrast.

CHAPTER 2

MAKING A SIMPLE FRAME

The basic wood-cutting, joinery, and matcutting skills needed to make a simple frame are elementary and can be learned in an afternoon. Obviously, practice will improve your technique, and once you have gained competence and confidence, you can attempt more complex joinery as and when needed.

The primary consideration at the outset is accuracy of measurement. Well-cut and measured pieces of wood fit together effortlessly. It is always possible to force badly cut joints together and to fill resulting cracks and holes, but the frames are never satisfactory. Even the unpracticed eye picks up a very small discrepancy in the squareness of a frame when it is hung on a wall. Also, if the frame is not square, then the mat, glass, and backing board all have to be cut with the same error to fit the frame. You can minimize this type of mistake by double checking before joining the frame together.

Esthetic considerations, however, are equally important. However well a frame is made, it will not be satisfactory unless it performs its other function, which is that of enhancing the image. There are many different ways to frame a picture, and a large variety of moldings and matboards available, so it is wise to take time in deciding which style best suits the picture. Professional framemakers will have samples on hand, but this is seldom a possibility for the home framemaker, so until you gain experience, you will find it helpful to take the picture with you when you choose mats and moldings.

CUTTING THE MAT

First check that the matboard is square. If it has come directly from a manufacturer or supplier, it is bound to be; but if you are using a cut off, it is essential to check. This is done by measuring the diagonals. If there is a discrepancy and it is not obvious where it is, a new right angle must be established and all subsequent measurements taken from this.

Give some thought to the proportions of mat to picture, as you don't want it to appear either swamped or crowded. It is usual to allow a larger margin at the bottom than at the sides and top. This is to correct an optical illusion which occurs when the picture is hung on the wall: if all the margins are the same width, the bottom one looks smaller than the others. A minor adjustment is all that is necessary, but some frame-makers prefer to have a considerably larger margin at the base of the picture for reasons of presentation. This is a matter of personal taste.

Cutting the window
It is a straightforward matter to cut a window with squared edges, but most mats are cut with beveled edges, which looks more attractive.

In the past, bevels were cut with a sharp knife and a steel straight edge, but this is not easy, which is why there are now so many mat cutters on the market. Most of these work on a similar principle, with one or two variations. The Dexter and other similar hand-held cutters have blades which are pushed along a straight edge, and are designed so that you can cut on the reverse of the matboard to avoid damage to the front surface. The measurements are also marked on the reverse. When cutting on the reverse, start the cut at the bottom left corner and continue clockwise around the matboard (if you were cutting on the front, you would start at the bottom right corner and work counterclockwise).

If you prefer to use the traditional knife and straight-edge method, try to find a small, sharp knife that feels comfortable in your hand. There is a large selection of craft knives available in tool and art supply stores.

Hold the knife as you would a pen, with the back of the blade resting against the bevel of the straight edge. Pierce the window in the corner with the point of the blade. Do not go too deep, and try to cut through the matboard in one pass. It is easier to first make a pilot cut, just lightly scoring the matboard, and then cut through in one or two passes after that. If you are cutting on the reverse of the matboard you will need to overcut the corners by the depth of the matboard. When all the sides have been cut, any rough areas can be smoothed with fine sandpaper.

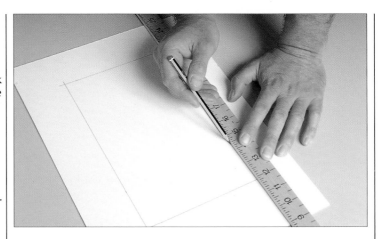

Using a matcutter
1 Before you measure the mat, put the picture on the board and move it around until you find the right margin width. Cut the outside measurement for the board and then mark the dimensions for the window.

2 Double-check all the measurements, and make sure the window is square at the corners by measuring the diagonals. The Dexter matcutter used here cuts $\frac{1}{32}$ in (0.7 mm) away from the straight edge, so another mark is made to make sure that the cutter is correctly aligned. If you use a different matcutter, read the instructions carefully before you begin.

3 When cutting on the back of the matboard, as here, the window must be overcut at the corners by the thickness of the board. Press the cutter through the board, line the straight edge up to the mark, and slowly move the cutter along the line, working clockwise around the mat from the bottom left-hand corner.

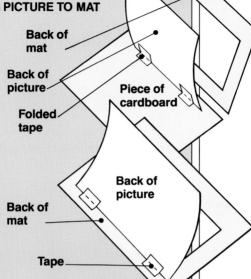

SECURING PICTURE TO MAT

▶ If you cut another piece of matboard the same size as the mat, you can attach the picture to it by making a hinge from small pieces of gummed or acid-free tape.

▶ However, the picture can be attached directly to the back of the mat, as shown here. Use as little tape as possible; the glass and backing board will hold the mat and picture in place.

Back of mat

Back of picture

Folded tape

Piece of cardboard

Back of mat

Back of picture

Tape

4 Before removing the piece cut for the window, make sure that it is not sticking anywhere, or you may tear it. The Dexter cutter will go through the board with one push, but with other types you may need to make two or three shallow cuts. When the window is complete, any rough edges can be smoothed with fine-grade sandpaper.

Using a knife
To cut beveled windows in the traditional manner with a knife and straight edge requires some practice, as well as a sharp-bladed knife that is comfortable to hold. When cutting on the reverse of the mat, work from the inside, placing the straight edge on the line marked for the top of the window, with the bulk of the board toward you. Make a series of cuts, remembering to overcut the corners by the thickness of the board.

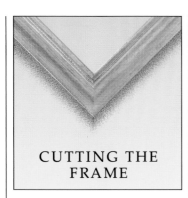

CUTTING THE FRAME

Both ends of each piece of molding must be cut at a 45° angle so that each corner fits together to form 90° (called a miter joint). The other requirement is that the opposite sides are precisely equal in size; if there are discrepancies, the corners will not fit tightly, and the frame will be weak.

Accurate measuring is thus very important. To calculate the frame size, first measure the picture size, or if the outside edge of a matboard is being used, the external mat size. Next measure the width of the back of the molding, not including the rabbet*. These two measurements, the image or mat size and the width of the molding, provide the formula for measuring the frame size, which is simply the image or mat size plus twice the width of the back edge of the molding, plus a small allowance for a comfortable fit (about $1/8$ in/3 mm). These measurements refer to the outer edge of the molding.

Cutting the frame
This procedure is the same whether you are using a simple wood or metal miter box or the more sophisticated miter saws. Not all moldings can be held in the same

manner. For example, a swept shape with a high outside edge is most easily held with the edge at the back of the box or miter saw, while a reverse-style molding with a low outside edge is easier to secure if the edge is toward you as you cut and the rabbeted edge securely held against the back.

Whichever way you decide to hold the molding, the bottom must always be in contact with the surface of the box or saw. If it is tilted, the angle of the cut will not be correct. When you have a long length of molding or a wide or awkward piece to cut, you may need to clamp the wood with C-clamps.

First cut the miter at one end of the molding, and then measure from that cut. Mark off on the long edge of the frame, and then use a try square to mark a perpendicular line down the outside edge. Make the next cut on this line.

When you have cut the first side, you can use it as a template for your next measurement, repeating the same procedure for the opposite pair of sides. Finally, compare the opposite sides face to face to make sure that the cuts are accurate. If you have access to a trimmer*, any small errors can be corrected easily; otherwise, adjustments can sometimes be made with a miter saw. In some cases, however, where the error is too small to trim with a saw, you may have to cut another piece of molding.

✱FURTHER INFORMATION

The parts of the
  molding   page 19
Saws and cutters   page 12

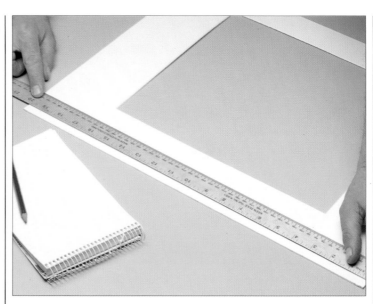

1 The frame can be made before the mat is cut, but it is easier and more reliable to take the measurements from the mat. Make a note of them as you measure, as it is easy to make mistakes.

2 Cut the first miter and then mark the position for the other one with a pencil mark on the outer edge of the frame, double-checking before cutting. Never try to measure a whole length for cutting; mark and cut one strip at a time.

3 The miter saw should be clamped to a workbench or sturdy table so that there is not too much movement as you cut. Place the molding in the saw, making sure that the bottom edge of the frame is resting on the cutting surface. Use the saw gently; a slow motion will yield more accurate cuts than a fast and furious attack.

6 Before joining (see following pages), the ash molding is stained to harmonize with colors in the picture. This can be done after joining, but it is easier to apply the stain when the wood is in separate pieces. After joining you may need to smooth the corners with sandpaper, and this will damage the stain.

4 When all the lengths have been cut, place each pair face to face to check the accuracy of the cuts. If there is a serious discrepancy, you can recut the miter, but it is seldom possible to remove an amount smaller than about $\frac{1}{8}$ in (3 mm).

5 Do not sandpaper the cut ends, as this will round them and prevent them from joining properly. Rough edges can be removed with a knife or chisel.

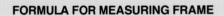
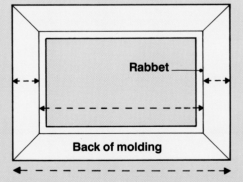

FORMULA FOR MEASURING FRAME

Rabbet

Back of molding

This diagram of the back of a finished frame shows how, by adding the measurements of the two back edges to the picture size, you can measure the outside dimensions of the frame. Remember not to include the rabbet in the measurements.

JOINING THE FRAME

Professional framemakers use a machine called an underpinner, or joiner, which glues and pins the frame in one operation in a matter of minutes. These were developed in response to the rapid growth of the industry in pre-decorated moldings. Some of these have high-gloss surfaces and elaborate color finishes which makes it difficult to disguise nail holes in the sides or the slightly rougher edges of hand-cut miters.

Joiners are now becoming less expensive, but most home framers will have to join the frame by hand, first gluing and then nailing the corners. To hold the frame firmly while the glue is drying, you will need some form of clamping jig, and there are now several types available, which join and tighten all four corners of the frame at the same time. In the past, framemakers used to make the frame in two halves, joining each opposite pair of pieces in a vice and nailing them at the same time as gluing. With modern clamps, the frame is left until the glue is dry and then nailed. It is possible to improvise a clamping jig from rope, or better still, rubber inner tubing or strong elastic, which can be tied around the frame and wedged with wooden blocks for greater tension.

Some molding shapes, such as reverse moldings, which have very shallow back edges, are inclined to jump out of a clamping jig, because there is insufficient surface to hold the frame in place. Spring miter clamps can be useful here, but they must be used with caution on predecorated moldings because they leave marks in the corners where the sharp teeth have bitten into the wood.

Nailing and filling

For small frames, wire brads are adequate, but as the size of the frame increases, so should that of the nail. As a rough rule-of-thumb, 1 in (2.5 cm) brads should be used for 1 in (2.5 cm) moldings, 2 in (5 cm) finishing nails for 2 in (5 cm) moldings, and so on.

The nails should be first hammered and then punched in and the holes filled with either a commercial wood putty or one made from glue and the fine sawdust from your miter saw. The advantage of this homemade filler is that it will provide a perfect color match, so if you are using natural wood that you intend to wax or stain, it is ideal.

Finally, the corners should be sanded to smooth the outer edges of the joints, after which the frame is ready to be decorated in any way you choose, or left as natural wood with a coat of varnish or French polish.

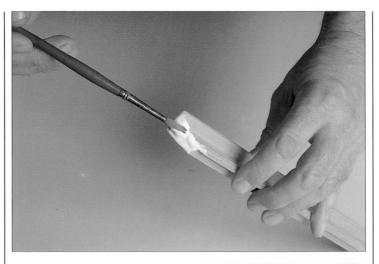

1 Before clamping, white wood glue is applied to the cut ends. It is strong and quick drying, and is now the adhesive most commonly used for all woodwork, though animal glues, epoxy resins, and casein glues can also be used. Make sure that the rabbet is covered with glue, as well as the main part of the frame. When the frame is in the clamp, excess glue can be removed with a damp rag.

2 These all-in-one clamps exert pressure evenly around the frame and are easy to operate. This is a plastic clamp with plastic tape, which is strong enough for most frames. Put the four sides of the frame together on a flat surface and position the corners before tightening the strap to take up the slack. Push the small levers out. These act as a brake so that the final tightening can be done with the handle on the main body.

3 A soft wood such as pine can be nailed through without drilling; you will only need an awl to make a pilot hole. Hardwoods, however, need to be drilled first, as otherwise the frame could fall apart with the impact of the hammer. With the frame supported in a vise, use a drill the same size as your nails, and penetrate the wood a little less than the depth of the nail.

5 When the nails have been driven two-thirds of the way in, use a nail set to knock them in fully. This protects the frame from hammer blows. Punch the nails a little below the surface so that the holes can be covered. Some nail sets have recessed heads that fit over the head of the nail; they are the easiest to use.

4 On small frames, one nail in each corner is adequate, but larger frames will need two or more. These are often nailed from each side so that the nails cross, providing extra strength.

6 After the nails have been punched in, the small holes should be filled with wood putty, which can be bought in a choice of colors to match the wood used. When the filler is dry, the corners are smoothed with sandpaper, but take care not to use too much pressure or the edges will become rounded.

CUTTING THE GLASS

Although most home framemakers will prefer to go to their local glass shop and have pieces of glass cut to size, it is useful to know how to cut and trim glass. If you make a mistake and find that the glass does not quite fit the frame, you can cut it down and use it for another frame. Glass is too expensive to waste.

There are three main types of glass cutter: diamond-headed (used for heavy-duty glass), tungsten, and steel wheel-headed cutters, the latter being the most commonly available. They normally have six or more wheels mounted on a wooden shaft. When a wheel becomes blunt, it can be rotated so that a new one takes its place. Even so, they do not last very long. Tungsten wheels, which are not much more expensive, last far longer.

For most frames $\frac{1}{16}$-inch glass, which is light and reasonably strong, is used. For very large areas of glass in a frame, you may have to buy either heavy duty ($\frac{1}{8}$ inch) glass or plexiglass. Beyond a certain size, approximately 3 feet (1 m) square, light glass is difficult to hold and can wobble in the middle and break. Thicker glass is more rigid.

1 Glass can be measured in the normal way with a ruler and T-square, but in this case the frame has already been joined, so the glass is held against the back of the frame and marked with a felt-tip pen.

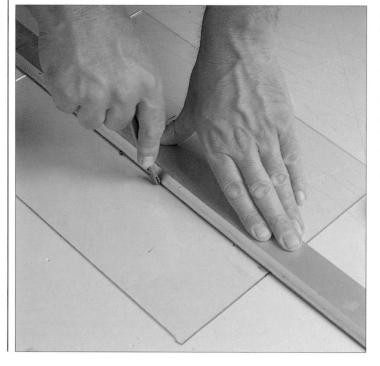

2 Make sure the cutting surface is smooth, as any lumps or bumps underneath will shatter the glass as you cut. Place a steel straight edge, preferably with a non-slip bottom, on the line. Lubricate the wheel in oil, mineral spirits or denatured alcohol, and score the glass. Practice on some scrap glass first so that you find out how much pressure to apply.

CUTTING AN OVAL

1 There are professional oval and circle cutters, but they are too expensive for occasional use. Here an oval cardboard template is used to guide the cutter around the curve.

2 Once the glass has been scored all the way around, tap vigorously with the other end of your glass cutter to loosen the oval shape from the surrounding glass.

3 If scoring and tapping does not release the oval, make a series of cuts from the edge of the oval to the outside edge of the glass. These sections can then be broken piece by piece around the oval.

3 Most pictures are framed with standard ¹⁄₁₆ in (2 mm) glass, which does not require a lot of pressure. After scoring, tap vigorously along the line of the cut. This makes it easier to break the glass cleanly. Many cutters have a round knob at the end of the handle for this purpose.

4 It is important to score the glass only once. If you recut over your last scored mark, the glass may break unevenly, and you will blunt the wheel. Here the glass is held with a thumb on each side of the scored line, and pressure is exerted from both sides. The glass should break easily.

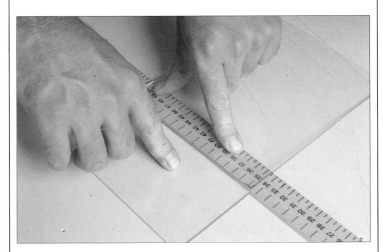

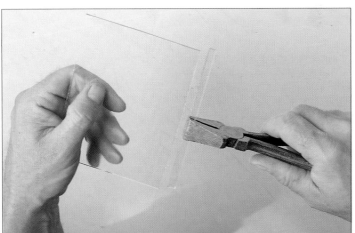

5 Another method of breaking glass, which is safer than holding it in your hands, is to place it on a flat ruler or straight edge and press either side. The scored mark must be very closely aligned to the edge of the ruler before downward pressure is exerted.

6 Sometimes the glass needs to be trimmed. Small pieces cannot be broken in the same way because there is not enough surface area, so special glass-breaking pliers are used, placed on the score line. If the glass does not break in one long piece, persevere along the cut, breaking off small sections at a time.

FINAL
ASSEMBLY

Once all the component parts of the frame are ready, the only task that remains is to cut a backing board from masonite, plywood, or thick cardboard. Masonite is probably the best choice, as plywood must be cut with a saw and tends to splinter at the edges. To cut masonite, mark the cutting line, score it on both sides with a sharp knife, and then break it.

It may be necessary to bevel the edges of the masonite at the back so that it fits into the frame; some predecorated moldings are too shallow to accommodate the "sandwich" of glass, picture, and backing board. This can be done with either a plane or a rasp.

Before assembling the frame, make sure that the glass is thoroughly clean on both sides and that there are no marks on the front of the mat. If there are, clean them off with a soft eraser. Attach the picture to the back of the mat with acid-free tape or brown gummed tape, which can be removed if necessary.

Place the frame upside down on a clean, flat surface, put the glass into it, and attach brown gummed tape to the outer edges of the glass so that it is hidden by the rabbet. This acts as a barrier to prevent dust from entering.

Put the mat and picture into the frame, and finally the backing board, then pick up the whole assembly and turn it around to check that the image and mat are centrally placed and that there is no dust trapped behind the glass.

To secure the backing board, small nails need to be hammered into the inner edges of the frame to hold the package together. If the wood is very hard, you will find it easier to make small pilot holes with an awl. Professional framemakers have point drivers that shoot flat points into the edges of the frame. These machines do save a lot of time, particularly if you have a lot of frames to assemble.

Finally, to prevent dust from entering from the back, apply more masking tape to cover the joint between the backing board and the frame.

1 This photograph shows the component parts of the finished frame: the wooden molding of stained ash; $\frac{1}{16}$ in (2 mm) picture glass; an ivory window mat with the print attached, and a backing board of masonite.

2 The glass is fitted into the frame and secured with gummed tape to prevent dust from entering from the front. Be careful with the placing of the tape; it should cover the side of the frame and only the thin margin of glass covered by the rabbet.

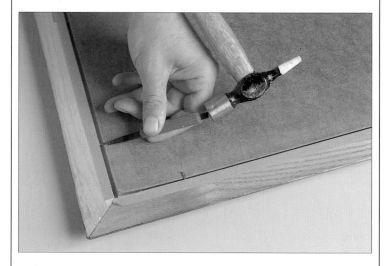

3 The mat with the picture attached is put in place, followed by the backing board, which is secured by nailing small panel pins around the frame. These can be driven in with a nail set, but this is not essential. Take care not to aim the hammer downwards, or you could break the glass.

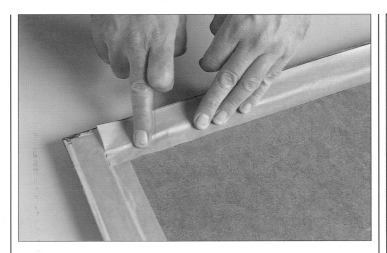

4 To seal the whole unit thoroughly and prevent any dust entering, the small gap between the backing board and the frame should be sealed with brown gummed tape.

Never use masking tape, as it will begin to peel off after quite a short time.

5 The back should look as neat and presentable as the front. Trim the gummed tape neatly, and if the backing board level is lower than the back of the frame, make a small cut in the tape so that it lies as close as possible to the frame.

6 Screw eyes for hanging should be placed approximately a quarter of the way down the frame and screwed firmly into the molding. Finally, brass wire is tied to both screw eyes and tightened. Nylon cord can also be used.

HARDWARE FOR HANGING

1 Brass screw eyes
2 Nylon cord
3 Double picture hooks and nails
4 Mirror plates
5 Chain
6 Chrome screw eyes
7 Single picture hooks and nails
8 Picture rail hooks
9 Picture wire

There are many ways to hang frames and a variety of hardware can be obtained. The simplest are screw eyes in various sizes, which are screwed into the back of the frame. These should be placed approximately a quarter of the height of the picture away from the top of the frame. If they are placed any farther down, the picture will hang at an angle from the wall. Brass wire or strong nylon cord can be attached between these two eyes, and the frame is then hung from picture hooks, hidden behind the frame. An alternative is to attach lengths of cord or chain and hang the frame from a picture rail.

For heavy frames, hanging plates, sometimes called mirror plates, are often used. These are screwed to the frame and the wall, and generally have two holes for screws into the frame and one hole for a screw into the wall. There are also hanging plates that fit flush so that no screws are visible from the front. They are keyhole shaped and are screwed to the back of the frame. At the top of the keyhole, a small hole is drilled so that it can hang on a wall screw.

CHAPTER 3

ADVANCED CARPENTRY

M ost frames are made with mitered corners, because decorative moldings look more attractive when the molding profile is continuously maintained around the corners of the frame. From a structural point of view, however, the miter joint has an obvious limitation. There is no connecting wood across it, and it is necessary to rely on glue and nails for strength.

There are ways in which the miters can be reinforced, but there are also frames that do not need miters, and where stronger structural joints can be used. This chapter discusses more unusual and complex frames, and their underlying structures.

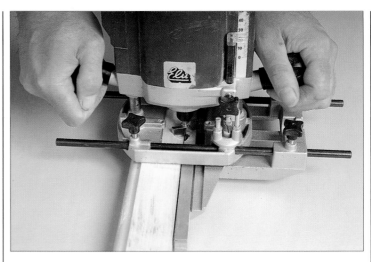

HOMEMADE PROFILES

In spite of the large numbers of different molding designs now available, it can sometimes be impossible to find the perfect shape for a particular frame. This problem can be solved either by making your own moldings using a router or combination plane, or by buying flat sections of wood and decorative beading and gluing them together.

Combination planes, or multiplanes, are essentially groove- and rabbet-cutting planes with extra cutters for decorations such as flutes and reeds. Although they have largely been replaced with the faster and more versatile routing power tools, they are still manufactured.

Routers are becoming increasingly used by home-based carpenters, both to cut molding, and for grooving and rabbeting work. They are fast and quite easy to use, and their popularity has kept their prices competitive.

For those framemakers without the facilities or means to use elaborate hand and power tools, there is still the option to make original profiles by combining existing wood shapes bought from local lumber yards and home centers. Many attractive frames can be made in this manner.

Using a router
1 To cut out a rabbet, set the cutting head to the required depth and push the router smoothly along the wood section. It is also possible to cut a rabbet after the frame has been assembled.

2 Routers can be fitted with a large variety of edge-forming cutters. Here, a beading cutter is pushed along the edge of the molding to create a round edge with a shallow groove on each side. Other common edge cutters include chamfer, ogee, and cove shapes. There is also a range of cutters for decorating the top surface of the frame, from simple grooves to more elaborate shapes.

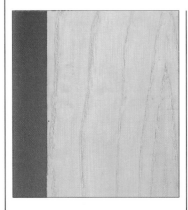

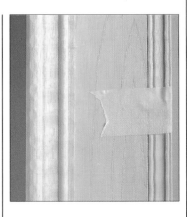

Composite profiles
1 A flat piece of ash is chosen as the central border of the frame. In this case, a 3 in (7.5 cm) section of ash-veneered plywood was cut from a large sheet.

2 To create a rabbet, a reeded section of wood was glued onto one edge of the border. It was fastened with masking tape to keep it in place while the glue hardened and nailed to the central border with thin veneer pins to give a strong joint.

3 A section of reeded wood, wider than the rabbet, but following a similar pattern, was then glued and nailed to the outside of the central margin. Many simple shapes of beading can be obtained from home centers and used in combination in this way.

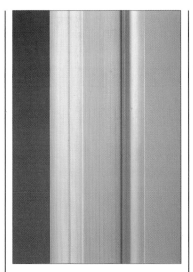

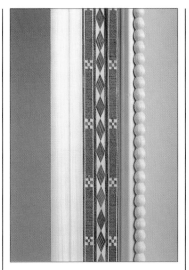

Veneer bandings
1 Wood veneers can be used to decorate frames, either as an overall covering or as a border. The underlying molding must be plain and almost flat, as veneers cannot be bent over a complex shape. Here a "windsor" profile, which has a flat central border, has been chosen.

2 A veneer banding was laid onto the flat border next to the outside edge, and another one of a different design was laid next to it. These bandings, which are made in a variety of designs and colors, are chiefly used for the decoration of small pieces of furniture and musical instruments.

3 The third piece of banding, the same design as the first, was aligned so that the patterns are parallel. The traditional method of attaching bandings is to chisel out a flat groove so that the banding lies flush with the rest of the wood, but in this case the three bandings fit exactly into the flat margin of the molding, so it was not necessary.

4 To complete the decoration, a strip of machine-carved beads was glued to the sight edge. It is easier to glue the decorative bandings and sections of wood before cutting the frame. Glue them to the wood molding and strap them tightly with masking tape to make sure that they lie flat and straight.

Wood beads
This strip of machine-cut beads was first gilded with imitation leaf and is now glued to the sight edge of a stained-oak molding. The gilt finish on the beads is protected from the masking tape by using strips of paper as a barrier.

VARIOUS JOINTS

There are a number of stronger joints than miters. These are most often used for frames with flat, undecorated wood sections, and are particularly useful for flat borders within a cassetta-style* frame or for box* frames.

A lap joint is one in which the plain end of one side is set into a rabbeted cut in the other, and it can look attractive in a natural wood finish. Although stronger than a miter or simple butt joint, it does still need to be pinned.

Corner halving joints are similar in principle and also need to be glued and reinforced using screws or dowels. The lapped miter is a more elegant version of the same joint, but has only half the overlap, and is consequently weaker. Both these halving joints are useful for frames with integrated borders and are considerably stronger than the simple miter joint. The photographs show various other options.

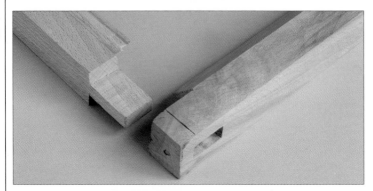

Mortise and tenon joint

1 This is a very strong joint and is used for furniture as well as framemaking. It requires accurate cutting for a tight fit and neat appearance.

2 Here the mortise has been pushed through the tenon, but not yet glued. The excess wood is marked for cutting.

3 This photograph shows the construction of the joint, with the mortise and tenon both cut. The excess wood, marked with pencil, will be cut away before joining and gluing.

4 The joint has been used for a "window" style frame in beech with a plain beveled section at the base and an ogee decoration on the other three inner edges.

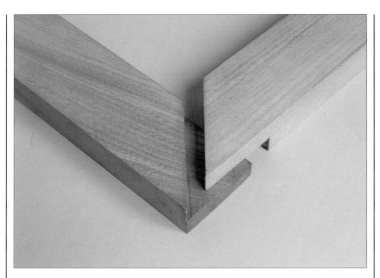

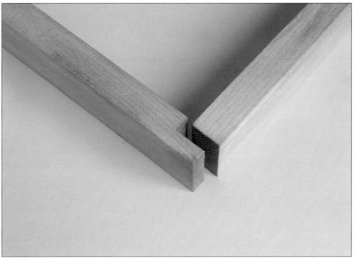

Lapped miters

1 These crossed joints are difficult to make, but look very attractive on natural-wood frames. The miter is strengthened by the lapped halves of the wood, which can be glued and nailed in the normal way. Precise cutting of the excess wood is essential for a tight joint.

Corner halving joint

These joints are similar in principle to the simple lap joint. They can be cut using a hand saw, and need to be glued and pegged or nailed. They are stronger than conventional miters and are often used on the central margins of cassetta-style frames.

2 Mark a line on the rabbeted side a half or a third of the width of the wood. Using the other side as a template, mark another line on the inner face and the top and bottom edges.

Indicate the excess with a pencil, and cut the two lines as neatly as possible. Glue and clamp together and nail through the rabbeted side.

REINFORCING MITER JOINTS

A more modern method of reinforcing miter joints is biscuit joining. The biscuit joiner is a miniature saw that cuts small grooves across joints. A "biscuit" of compressed beech spread with white or yellow glue is inserted into the groove, and the glue causes the biscuit to expand inside the joint, making a strong bond.

On many old frames, you will find that, although the glue has deteriorated, the miters are still strong, due to a traditional method of reinforcement. The mitered corners are glued and pinned in the normal manner, and then a channel is cut across the miters and a wedge inserted.

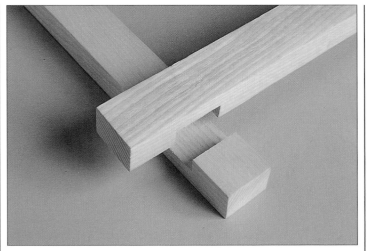

Crossover frames

1 Mark the dimensions of the picture size on the back of the wood and add the required length of the crossover. Indicate the excess wood sections on all crossover sides, and then saw both edges of the cut-out piece. The excess can then be knocked out cleanly with a sharp chisel. The rabbet can be cut with a power router or a plow plane. If a plane is used, it is easiest to make the rabbet before the frame is assembled, but a router with a right-angle fence can cut it after joining, and rounded corners can be cut square with a chisel.

Rustic crossovers

1 This more traditional crossover frame, also for a sampler, is made of oak. It is made in the same way as the limed ash frame, with the excess wood being cut and chiseled out of the molding.

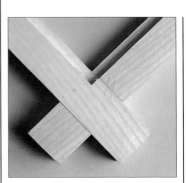

2 After gluing, the crossovers can be pegged with wooden dowels, or nailed from the back for greater strength. There are no fixed rules for the proportions of the crossover sections, but in general they do not usually exceed a quarter of the frame's length.

3 A small flower ornament has been molded from composition (see page 136) as a decorative boss for the corners of the frame.

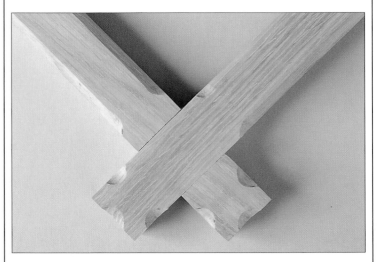

2 The sides of the frame are decorated with stopped chamfer cuts, which are repeated on the crossover sections. These can be made with a sharp chisel or with a router. This type of decoration is well suited to an unsophisticated subject such as a cross-stitch embroidery.

3 The frame has been used to display a child's sampler. The thick oak section has stopped chamfer decorations on the sides and at the crossed corners. It has been stained a darker color to give the appearance of mature oak. A gilded slip has been added to keep the sampler away from the glass.

ORNAMENTAL EXTENDED CORNERS

This ornamental device, in which the decorative molding is extended at the corners to form squares outside the main frame, has been used in many ways since the Renaissance. Although the style is usually associated with period frames, it can be equally striking used with modern moldings.

With careful measuring, all the cuts can be carried out using a simple miter saw, but the cuts must be absolutely precise. If the opposite sections of the extended corners are not identical, the frame will look lopsided and unsightly.

In spite of the difficulties, it is well worth persevering with ornamental corners, as you can vary the basic idea to make many different styles. For example, some overmantel frames are constructed with extended corners at the top and ordinary miter joints on the bottom, which gives an attractive top-heavy appearance to the frame.

1 The sides of the frame are cut in the normal way, and then each end is re-cut across the miter in the opposite direction, starting at the top of the sight edge.

2 To form the extended corners, two triangles of wood are cut for each corner. Each triangle should be the smallest possible section of complete molding, with two 45° cuts from the sight edge. When glued together, they form 90° at the extended corner. Bind them with masking tape or use a spring miter clip to hold them in place while the glue dries.

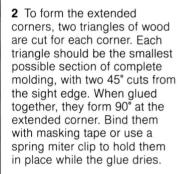

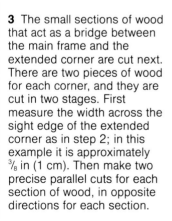

3 The small sections of wood that act as a bridge between the main frame and the extended corner are cut next. There are two pieces of wood for each corner, and they are cut in two stages. First measure the width across the sight edge of the extended corner as in step 2; in this example it is approximately $\frac{3}{8}$ in (1 cm). Then make two precise parallel cuts for each section of wood, in opposite directions for each section.

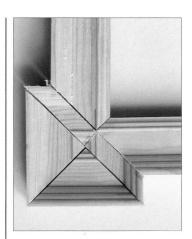

4 The second cut is made across the miter on the rabbet of the small sections of wood. This has to be done delicately because the rabbet is liable to break off the frame with the pressure of the saw. This second cut should allow the bridge sections to align neatly with the extended corners. Glue and bind them with masking tape to the extended corners.

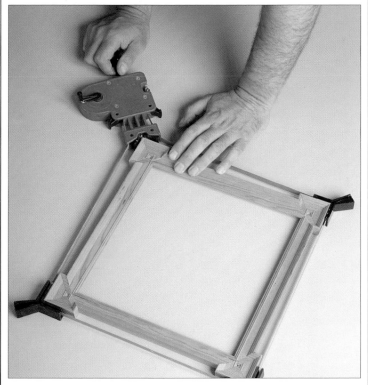

▲ This frame is one of a pair made by Michele Riley for two 17th-century prints. The frames have been painted with a thick black casein paint, and the top line of the sight-edge groove decoration has been picked out in an ivory color, emphasizing the extended corner decorations.

5 To join the frame, first glue the main frame together. This is tricky because there is only a narrow joining edge. Once the glue has set, place the extended corners in the same clamp, place them to the main frame and tighten the clamp.

The protruding corners are vulnerable to knocks, so to strengthen them, glue and nail small plates of wood or masonite to the back of the frame.

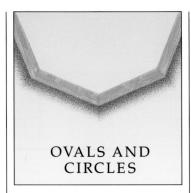

OVALS AND CIRCLES

Oval and circular frames, both of which are often used for mirrors, are nowadays usually cut with specialist machinery. The moldings are cut on a curve and then joined – usually in four pieces – into the finished shape. However, they can also be handmade, using traditional methods.

Small frames can be turned on a lathe, but larger ones have always exercised the ingenuity of traditional framemakers. The method shown here, which involves gluing a series of pegs onto a board in the required shape* and winding strips of veneer around them, certainly dates back to the 18th century and probably earlier.

*FURTHER INFORMATION

Marking out an
oval   page 57

1 For this method, a wood-and-peg template is made first, with the shape marked by a series of pegs drilled and glued at intervals of approximately $\frac{1}{2}$ in (1.3 cm). Thin strips of veneer are measured to the desired depth of the frame and cut with a craft knife.
A few more strips are cut approximately $\frac{1}{4}$ in (6 mm) narrower to act as the rabbet.

2 The frame is constructed upside down so that the top surface lies flush with the template. A clothespin is used here to secure one end of the veneer strip to the outside of the pegs.

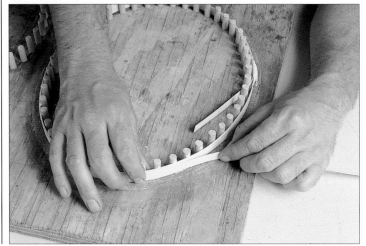

3 The veneer is then tightly wrapped around the pegs, and glue is applied in between each layer. It is important to keep the veneer flush with the pegs at all times, so that the correct shape is maintained.

6 Here gesso is used as an undercoat for a painted finish. This is thick enough to cover any small blemishes and also helps to bind the whole frame together.

4 The veneer is wound around the frame until the required thickness is reached. It will need approximately ten rounds to make an inch, with slight variations according to the thickness of the veneer.

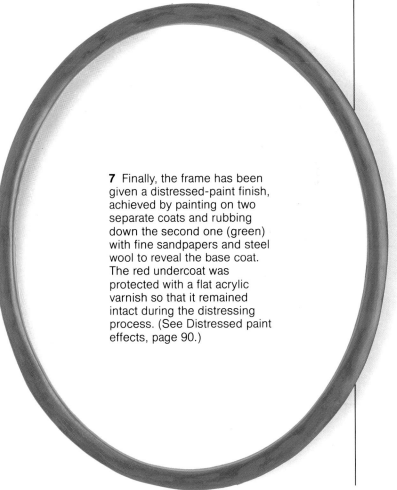

7 Finally, the frame has been given a distressed-paint finish, achieved by painting on two separate coats and rubbing down the second one (green) with fine sandpapers and steel wool to reveal the base coat. The red undercoat was protected with a flat acrylic varnish so that it remained intact during the distressing process. (See Distressed paint effects, page 90.)

5 When the frame has reached the required width, it is left to dry and set for a few hours. It can be secured with strips of masking tape. The many layers of veneer will leave a ridged surface on the frame, which can be smoothed with a plane and sandpaper.

SLIPS AND BOX FRAMES

Slip frames, which have an inner piece to isolate the picture from the glass, can either be used in a purely functional way to prevent the picture from sticking to the glass and causing damage, or as an extra decoration.

Slips can also be used as fillers for frames that are too large. They can be bought in many different shapes and finishes.

Box frames

These are mainly used to frame objects such as medals, jewelry, butterflies, and other small-scale items, but they can also create a dramatic effect for pictures, making them look as though they are in a presentation cabinet.

It is necessary to have molding deep enough to trap the glass at the front, leaving a gap between it and the artwork, which is secured at the base of the frame. The glass can be held in place with slips, either visible or hidden, which are attached to the sides of the frame.

There are some especially deep moldings manufactured for this purpose, but you can also modify existing moldings with an extra section of wood on the bottom.

Textile frames

1 This is the flat central border of a cassetta-style frame, which was covered with canvas, with gesso on top. It is now painted with indigo latex to contrast with the warm colors of the textile.

2 The inner frame was painted with shellac and bronze pigments before being fitted to the central border. This needs to be cut carefully to fit tightly inside the flat molding. It is possible to buy or make molding with a double rabbet for this purpose.

3 Finally, the outer frame of stained and varnished wood is fitted around the border piece. This both protects the inner frames and adds another color and shape to the composite frame. For extra security, the frames can be glued and nailed together.

4 The textile, which has been attached to a wooden panel, is fitted into the frame without glass. Glass can be used, and frequently is, since it protects the fabric from dust and dirt, but it can detract from the overall appearance, making it more difficult to see the fine stitched texture.

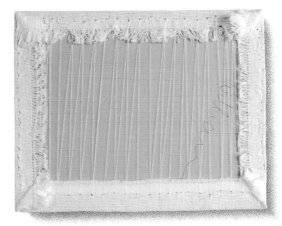

Stretching embroidery

Before framing stitched embroidery, it is sometimes necessary to stretch it. Robust fabric can be stretched in a similar way to artist's canvas, that is, nailed or stapled onto a wooden frame. For more delicate works, a backing board can be used as a support, and the fabric can be laced with thread across the back.

BOX FRAME CONSTRUCTIONS

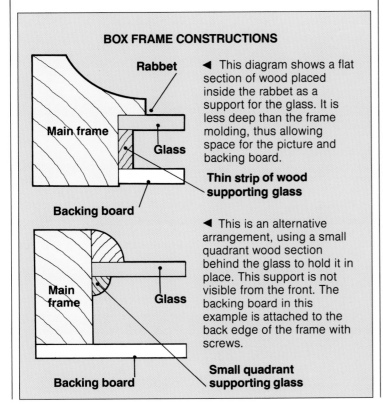

Rabbet

◄ This diagram shows a flat section of wood placed inside the rabbet as a support for the glass. It is less deep than the frame molding, thus allowing space for the picture and backing board.

Main frame

Glass

Thin strip of wood supporting glass

Backing board

◄ This is an alternative arrangement, using a small quadrant wood section behind the glass to hold it in place. This support is not visible from the front. The backing board in this example is attached to the back edge of the frame with screws.

Main frame

Glass

Backing board

Small quadrant supporting glass

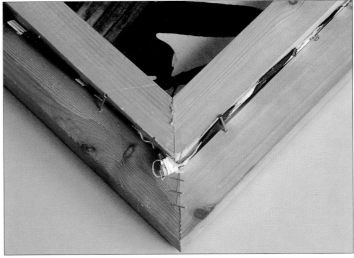

Quadrant slip

In this case a colorful batik on white muslin is separated from the glass by using a quadrant slip underneath the glass. The quadrant is the same type of wood as the outer frame and has been stained and polished to match. The photograph shows the reverse of the frame and the stretcher used to display the batik. These stretchers can be made from flat wood, but remember to chamfer the facing edges so that the fabric is not damaged by sharp corners.

Decorative slip

Slips can be used for purely decorative effect, as here, or to separate the glass from the picture. They are also used to pad out existing frames which are too large for a particular picture. They are available in many different shapes, sizes, and finishes, and are extremely useful for minor adjustments.

Cabinet style

1 This "shadow box" or cabinet-style frame is used to advantage to display a magnificent ivory fan. The frame is a deep, flat section of wood with small floral ornaments. The dark velvet background contrasts with the ivory and allows all the fine carving to be seen clearly.

2 Dark green velvet-covered slips hold the glass at the front of the box. The back panel of velvet with the ivory fan attached is held at the back of the frame in a rabbet formed by the slips and the outer frame. Movable fasteners hold the back panel in place.

FRAMES WITH AND WITHOUT RABBETS

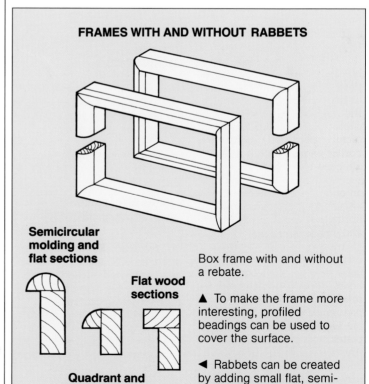

Semicircular molding and flat sections

Flat wood sections

Quadrant and flat sections

Box frame with and without a rebate.

▲ To make the frame more interesting, profiled beadings can be used to cover the surface.

◄ Rabbets can be created by adding small flat, semi-circular, or quadrant sections to plain timber.

FLOATING FRAMES

In this style of frame, the picture does not sit behind a rabbet in the normal way, but stands proud of its protective border. It is particularly effective with panel paintings or artwork where the image extends fully to the edges; because there is no rabbet, nothing is hidden.

There are a number of ways to approach the construction of this kind of frame. One is to build a border of wood or particle board around the edge of the painting. As in a mat, the width of this border is chosen to suit the picture. The picture is then secured to this border using a batton that is attached to both. Another section of wood or molding – an outer "frame" – can be attached to the edges of the border to give both protection and extra emphasis.

Another simple way to construct a floating frame is to cut a piece of flat wood or board to fit around the picture precisely, and then secure the picture from the back using blocks, batons, or reinforcing plates. The picture can be presented flush with the border, recessed, or projecting forward.

1 This portrait has been painted on a wooden panel, beveled at the edges. It is now attached to a background of oak-veneered plywood by gluing and then screwing it from the back.

2 Both the frame and the background have been sealed with shellac and then waxed, so that the warm, natural colors of the wood complement the warmer shades in the portrait.

FIXING PICTURE TO FRAME

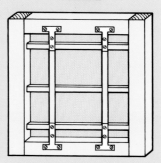

▲ This diagram shows the back of the floating frame shown on page 80. A simple wood section was constructed around a picture painted on a wooden panel. A framework of wooden struts was then attached to the back of the panel and attached to the frame with metal reinforcing plates.

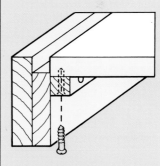

▲ This example shows a batten that has been glued and nailed onto a wooden margin, with a recess on the inside edge. The canvas stretcher support for the picture is then attached with screws to the batten.

PENTAGONS, HEXAGONS, AND OCTAGONS

On most miter saws* a simple protractor is provided with positions indicated for pentagons, hexagons, and octagons. They are no more difficult to cut than 45° miter joints. Some contemporary clamps have versatile corners which can accommodate the various angles, so that these frames can be glued and tightened in the same manner as conventional types. Alternatively, sprung miter clamps* can be used.

For pentagons, because of the uneven number of sides, each section of molding must be the same length, but hexagons and octagons can have different side lengths, provided the opposite sides are equal. In this way many interesting shapes can be made which are particularly attractive for mirrors and decorative work.

Pentagon
1 This shape was chosen for the five-pointed starfish for obvious reasons, though it can be an effective format for other shapes as well. Unlike octagons and hexagons, pentagons have to have equal-sized sides.

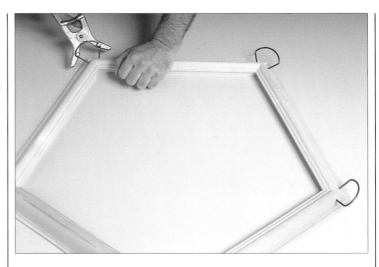

2 The frame was cut with a miter saw, set at 54°. The joinery is slightly tricky because the reverse-shaped molding will not fit into conventional clamps, so spring miter clips are used.

3 The frame was gessoed and painted with terracotta burnishing clay, after which a coat of black burnishing clay was applied on top and distressed with steel wool to reveal some of the red undercolor. This softens the black surface and picks out the red in the image.

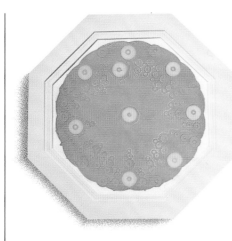

Octagon

1 Sometimes an image can benefit from a less conventional shape than the standard rectangle. This colored etching has an eight-sided window mat decorated with wash and pen lines. It is possible to vary the sizes of the sides of an octagon frame, but here all the sides are equal.

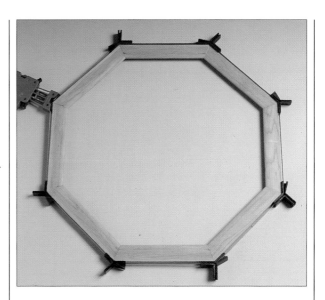

2 A frame of rounded oak molding has been cut in the same way as the pentagon, but with the saw set at an angle of 67°. For the joinery, an all-in-one clamp is used, with extra corner pieces.

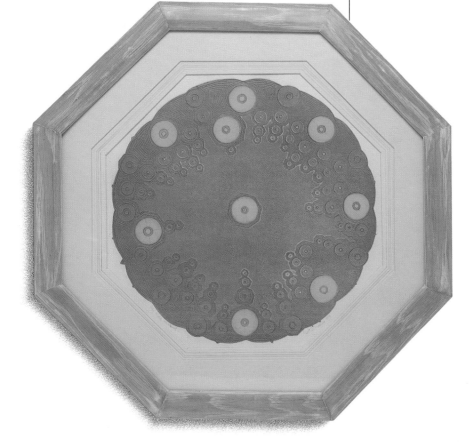

3 The oak frame has been pickled to make it more discreet in tone and prevent it from dominating the delicate colors of the print. Both frames and etchings are by Derek James.

CHAPTER 4

DECORATIVE MATS

Mats, which are usually made of cardboard and have bevel-edged windows, both present and protect works on paper, such as watercolors, prints, and drawings.

The cardboard acts as a barrier between the image and the glass, which is necessary because any moisture present in the atmosphere around the frame can make the glass cling to the paper and cause damage.

Mats were not widely used until the middle of the 19th century, when cardboard was industrially produced for the first time. Previously, works on paper had sometimes been protected from the glass by small pieces of wood, often the size of matchsticks, which were inserted into the rabbet of the frame behind the glass. Another device was to use a slip frame placed behind the glass and in front of the picture. This was usually a beveled flat section of wood, which was gilded or decorated to suit the picture. Both methods are still used today to present images where a mat seems inappropriate. Embroideries, for example, often need the protection of glass, but are not always suited by a window mat. Similarly, a window mat would not be the best choice for an old document, or any work in which the edges of the paper are an integral part of the overall image. For most pictures on paper, however, a mat is both the easiest and most attractive option.

PROPORTIONS

Whatever color or decoration you decide on for a mat, it will not be successful unless the margins are in pleasing proportion to the image. As mentioned earlier, it is usual to allow a greater depth of margin at the bottom of the picture, but apart from this there are no golden rules about the proportion of mat to picture; your choice will be affected by personal taste, prevailing fashions, and the color of the matboard. However, it is generally accepted that wide margins look better in neutral colors such as ivory or pale grays, as a large area of strong color around a picture can swamp it and interfere with our perception of it. It is useful to have a few pieces of board to put around the edges of the picture to see what seems to complement the image best.

Small images such as engravings or woodcuts often look more impressive in wide mounts, which add weight and importance to them. In a narrow margin, these small images can often be lost and unnoticed. On larger pictures a wide mount may look appropriate, but will sometimes make the overall size of the frame too big for displaying on a wall.

WORKING IT OUT

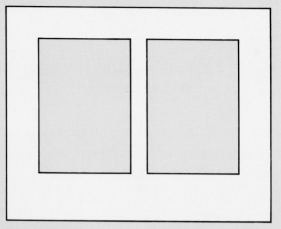

Double windows
When two pictures are framed together, for example two similar prints or paintings of the same subject, the central border needs to be quite narrow, approximately half the measurement of the top and side borders. This will separate the images while emphasizing their relationship.

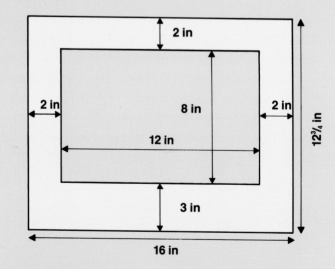

Making a cartoon
It is helpful to work out the proportions by making a "cartoon" like this. You can refer to it while you cut the mat, which will prevent mistakes.

Ovals and circles

Ovals and circles are trickier to mark out and cut than straight-sided windows, but both can be marked with a compass, as shown here.

The Dexter hand-held matcutter will cut both ovals and circles as long as you make a template, preferably of plywood or masonite. This should be slightly smaller than the required size (about $1/32$ inch) all around and can be cut with a bandsaw or knife.

Place the template on the face of the mount (it is not possible to cut on the reverse using this process), and secure it with nails or pins. Place the cutter tight against the edge of the template, with the blade piercing the board, and gently push it around the template. Circles are easier than ovals because the curve is constant; an oval changes curves as it approaches the apex, and it is easy to slide away from the edge of the template.

There are professional oval and circle cutters that are easy to use, but are too expensive for the home-based framemaker. In recent times a new hand-held oval and circle cutter has been developed by Daler, who manufacture matboard. This is an ingenious device, similar in principle to professional cutters, but smaller in size at a fraction of the price.

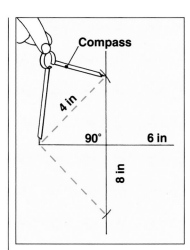

Marking an oval

1 Decide the width and height of the oval window required. Mark out both measurements, being careful to draw straight lines that intersect at 90°. Take half the measurement of the longest side. Mark the measurements onto the longest side from the end of the shortest side, using a compass.

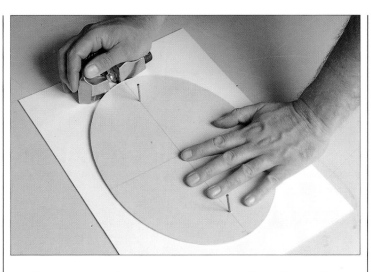

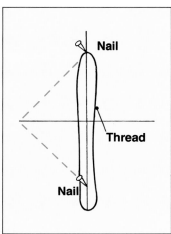

2 Hammer thin nails into the intersecting points of the measurements on the longest side. With a piece of string or some strong thread, make a loop around both nails. The loop should be tied at the outside of the long measurement and reach the farthest nail.

Cutting with a template
1 Here the method has been used to cut a template from stiff cardboard which has been nailed onto the matboard in the correct position. The Dexter cutter cuts $\frac{1}{32}$ in (0.7mm) away from the straight edge, so the template has to be cut that much smaller all around. It is not possible to cut on the back of the mat for this procedure.

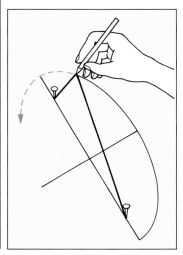

3 Place a pencil inside the loop and pull it tight. Then slowly push the pencil around the loop.

2 Place the cutter carefully against the template, and pierce the board with the blade. Push the cutter slowly all around the template, paying special attention to the change of curvature at the apex of the oval. When you have cut all around the oval, it should come out of the matboard easily. Any rough edges can be smoothed with fine-grade sandpaper.

DOUBLE AND TRIPLE MATS

Double and triple mats can enhance the presentation of the picture by adding greater depth and color possibilities. There are many variations of complementary and contrasting colors. Sometimes a color in the picture can be echoed in the thin margin of color that forms the inner border of a double mat, while on other occasions a contrasting color can be used for dramatic effect.

The conventional arrangement of proportions is that the inner mat or mats have the same margins on all sides, while the outer mat has a greater margin at the bottom. If you are using a bright color for an inner margin, it may be enough to have $\frac{3}{8}$ inch or less showing; any more might conflict with the picture.

Where there are many colors in the picture, or where there is no obvious predominant color, it may be safer to use neutral colors for the inner margins. Double mats can be very effective when both inner and outer mats are the same color, particularly when a neutral ivory or gray is used against a colorful pastel or watercolor. The bevels form slight shadows around the inner mat, giving a discreet hint of soft and subtle decoration.

Triple mats expand the possibilities of color variations; for example, you could use two shades of blue, gray, or ivory with a slip of bright red in the middle. Sometimes the inner mat is gilded or decorated with marbled paper, while the outer mat is left plain.

Double and triple mats do, of course, entail more work in the drawing and cutting, and you will need to measure very carefully. A small error of judgment on a single mat may escape attention, but on a double or triple one, any mistakes are amplified by the other windows. The inner mats need only be a little wider than the visible margins and can be taped to the back of the outer mat.

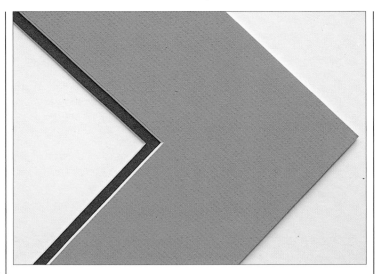

▲ A double mat enhances the presentation of a picture by adding depth. It also enables you to experiment with different color combinations. Here, two shades of blue are used, the darker one on the inside.

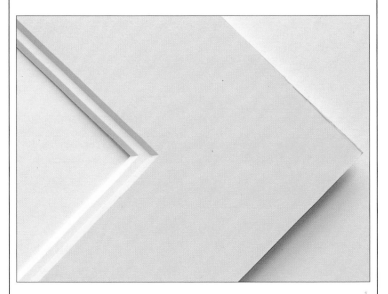

▲ In this example, two colors of matboard have been doubled in thickness to increase the size of the bevels. It is not difficult to glue two pieces of board together, and the joints are barely noticeable when the bevel has been cut.

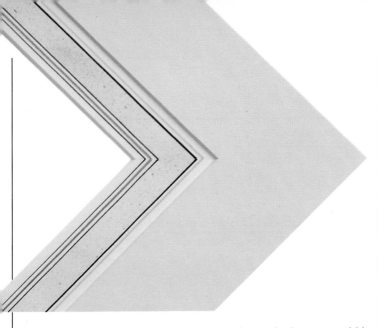

▲ This double mat has a decorative inner mat, wider than normal to accommodate the decoration. The "wash line" is actually an extra border of sprayed paint edged with gold lines. A margin the same width as the decoration was cut out of a piece of scrap board to act as a mask while the spraying was done.

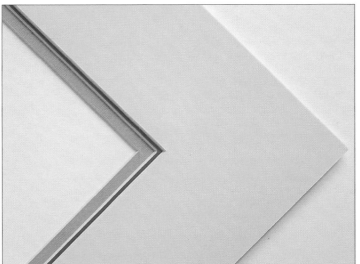

▲ In this triple mat, a thin slip of red is sandwiched between a gray and an ivory board. A bright color can be used in small quantities without interfering with the image. Great care must be taken in the measurements of double and triple mats because the slightest error shows up.

UNUSUAL SHAPES

Shaped windows can suit some pictures, particularly if the window echoes a contour in the image. They are more difficult to execute with hand-held cutters than standard mats, and templates have to be used for curves.

1 This simple device adds a little square decoration to the corners of the window aperture.

2 This decorative cut-out has another colored board used both as a double mat and as a background for the cuts.

3 The spraying method was used here to decorate the inner mount. The bevel was sprayed as well, and masks of right-angled triangles were placed at the corners to "reserve" white areas, which were then edged with a fine black line.

4 A complex shape of curves and straight lines are joined together and amplified with a decorative gold line.

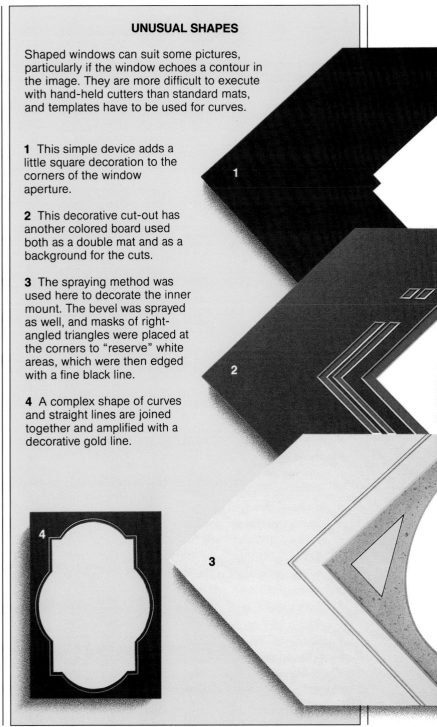

VARIETIES OF MATBOARD

Most matboard is made from wood pulp and faced with colored paper. A wide variety of colored and decorated boards is now available, ranging from flat colors to marbled, textured, and fabric effects. The more decorative boards tend to follow fashions in the world of interior design and change from time to time.

All industrially made mats, whatever the finish, will reveal a plain bevel when cut. This can be a pleasant contrast to the surface decoration, but you may prefer an overall color or texture that includes the bevel, in which case you must decorate the mat* yourself.

Board weight
The thickness of matboard is expressed in "ply" size, and the most generally available board is usually 4 ply. It is not always easy to find thicker board unless you go to a specialist supplier, but one way to make a heavier mat is to glue two sheets together before cutting. When the beveled window is cut, the joint is not obvious, and the extra depth of the bevel can be attractive. It is, of course, a little harder to cut through two matboards.

Conservation board
Unfortunately, much matboard is still made of unrefined groundwood pulp, which contains acids and can be harmful to works on paper. The "burning" by the acid takes place over a long period of time, so for temporary items such as posters or cheap prints it is not necessary to purchase the more expensive acid-free or acid-neutral board. For a picture, map, or document of any value, however, acid-free conservation board should always be used. The popularity of this has lowered the price and increased the color range in recent years, and conservation gummed tapes and glues have also been brought out to help preserve particularly valuable pictures.

✱FURTHER INFORMATION

Fabric mats	page 66
Special finishes	page 68
Broken color effects page	69

▶ Good-quality matboard and conservation board are now available in a choice of colors suitable for almost any subject. Textured boards are less easy to obtain, but for these effects you can glue textured paper or fabric onto plain board, or use the gesso method.

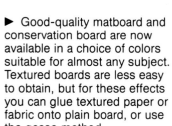

Gesso texture on mats
A thick mixture of gesso, as used for pastiglia decoration (see p.120), can be used to texture the matboard. It can be stippled on, giving an even, grainy surface, dabbed on for greater texture, or combed or scratched in patterns. It is best to use thick, high-quality matboard for this purpose, as thin cardboard may buckle and warp when the gesso dries.

LINE AND WASH TECHNIQUES

Line and wash is a traditional form of decoration associated with watercolors of the late 19th century and still used for watercolors and other works on paper.

The paint used for the wash line is watercolor, or sometimes thin gouache if an opaque or white line is required. The lines, too, are often watercolor, drawn on with a pen, though ink is also used. There are no golden rules for the divisions of space between the lines, but commonly the wash line is between ⅜ in (1 cm) and ¾ in (2 cm), and two or three pen lines are grouped very close together on each side. Picture framers who do a lot of this work usually make or buy an acetate or plexiglass corner with many pinholes to mark out the various dimensions. This can save a lot of time.

The wash

It is best to paint the wash line first and then edge the borders with a pen line, which gives a crisp quality to the edges. Watercolor is a difficult medium to work with, so if you are a beginner, make a few practice attempts on some scrap board until you get the feel of the paint. It helps to brush the area of the wash with clear water to dampen it, which encourages the color to settle evenly. Ox gall, a wetting agent used in the manufacture of watercolor, is a useful addition to the watercolor mix (a few drops added to the water is all you need).

Contrary to expectation, it is both easier and faster to brush the color on freehand than to use a ruler, but if you feel unable to try without a ruler, turn it upside down so that the bevel edge is on the bottom. This should prevent the ruler from picking up color and dragging it across the board.

It is necessary to brush over the line more than once to achieve a perfectly even wash, so begin with a dilute color and a brush of approximately the same width as the wash line. Pull the brush along the border, and keep on going around the wash line until the color is even and dark enough. Finally, go over the line with clear water and a clean brush, until all corners overlap and other irregularities are blended into the wash.

The pen line

When the wash line is dry, a pen is used with the same or a slightly darker color to sharpen the edges. There are many fine-nibbed, fiber-tipped graphic pens now available in a large range of colors which can be used, but the traditional implement is a lining pen. Gold and silver lines can be made by using either water-soluble metallic ink and a lining pen, or one of the gold or silver fiber tips available from most art supply stores.

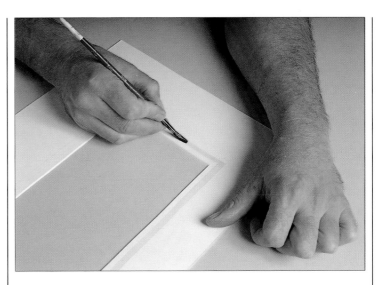

Wash lines
As long as you keep the paint wet, you can maintain control of it. Draw the border lightly in pencil and then wet the whole area within the pencil lines with clear water prior to painting.

Choose a brush the right size for the margin, and start to paint freehand around the mount. Keep going around until the wash line is blended, using clear water to even the paint as you work.

Pen lines
The traditional lining pen used here is versatile because it can be used with both watercolor and ink, and the lines can be thick or thin to suit the image. Mark the line in pencil first, and place a piece of paper at each end to prevent any deposited blobs of color marking the mat. Use a plexiglass ruler turned upside down so that the bevels are underneath. This raises it slightly off the mat so that there is no danger of smudging the color.

Gold paper lines
1 Gold lines are usually fairly thin, so you will either have to cut large sheets into narrow strips or buy thin strips of gold paper, available on rolls from specialist suppliers.

Gold acetate
Here, a gold line is made with gold leaf pressed onto acetate tape (used, among other things, for heat-stamping gold dates onto leather diaries). Cut the tape to the size of the longer side first, and then you can cut down the same piece to use on the shorter side. Mark the ends of the lines clearly, and use a pointed piece of wood (the end of a small paintbrush is ideal) to score a line. The bright gold side of the tape should be facing you.

Varieties of wash line
1 A double wash line was painted on this mat, with a slightly darker blue on alternate margins. A yellow and black pen line was drawn on the inner sight edge, and the same yellow used again on the outer edge.
2 Circular wash lines are no more difficult to paint than the conventional square or rectangular ones. This example has two pen lines on each side of the wash line, and for these you will need a pen mounted onto a compass, which can either be bought or improvised with a standard compass.
3 A fairly complex design is used for this wash line. The extended corners can add a flourish to the conventional colors and pen lines.

2 Indicate on the mat where the gold paper strip is to be attached. Cut the paper strip to size, and using a 45° angle, cut neat miters on the paper. It is now ready to be glued onto the mat using paper glue. Gold papers can be given a more "matured" look by painting ink or colored shellac on top.

1

2

3

DECORATIVE PAPERS

There are many styles of decorative paper which can be glued down on matboard. Some, like the marbled papers, are intensely colorful with dense, intricate patterns, while others are more discreet, with perhaps gold or colored flecks against a neutral ground. If you go to a specialist supplier, you will find hundreds of different types of paper, both hand- and machine-made.

There is no reason why wallpaper should not be used if you can find one of the appropriate pattern and thickness, but in general, you want a thin paper that will not stand out too much from the surface of the matboard. In recent years there has been a vogue for strips of marbled paper placed around the mats of prints, particularly botanical album prints and other decorative images. Marbled paper* is thin and has repeating patterns, so is ideal for this treatment.

Sometimes a whole mat can be covered with a decorative paper, but this can overwhelm the image, so it is more usual to restrict their use to border decorations. They can be used instead of a wash line, or for the inner margins of double and triple mats where rich decoration in small areas can contrast very well with plain colored matboard.

A plain but textured paper, however, can be effective used over the whole mat area. For example, good-quality textured rag watercolor paper glued onto board and then cut to expose the bevels in the window can look very attractive for prints and engravings that only require minimal decoration.

For sharp-edged line decoration in paper, it is most important to be neat and accurate. You will need a sharp craft knife, a ruler, and a triangular set square with two 45° angles, which will help you cut accurate miter corners in the paper. These look much neater than simple butt joins.

✳FURTHER INFORMATION

Making marbled
  papers   page 63

▶ The photograph shows a small selection of machine-made marbled papers, described as "elephanthide" and "marltone." They are quieter and less obtrusive than the papers shown on page 65, and could be used for a whole mat rather than just as a border.

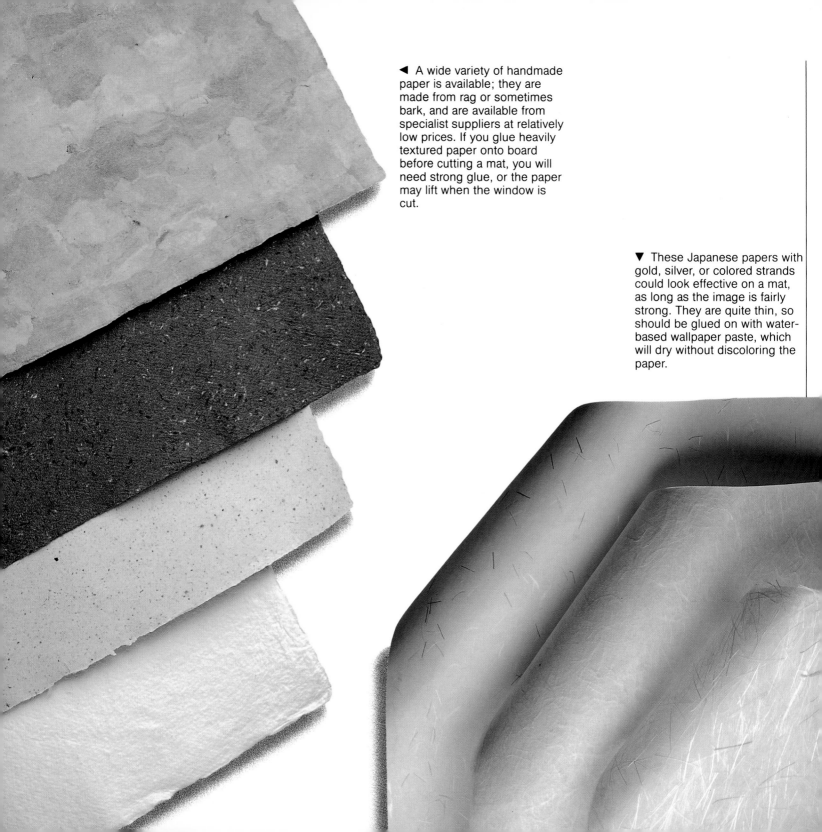

◄ A wide variety of handmade paper is available; they are made from rag or sometimes bark, and are available from specialist suppliers at relatively low prices. If you glue heavily textured paper onto board before cutting a mat, you will need strong glue, or the paper may lift when the window is cut.

▼ These Japanese papers with gold, silver, or colored strands could look effective on a mat, as long as the image is fairly strong. They are quite thin, so should be glued on with water-based wallpaper paste, which will dry without discoloring the paper.

MAKING MARBLED PAPERS

There are two ways to make marbled papers. The first uses oil paint diluted with mineral spirits, which is floated on a mixture of hot water and gelatin. The second uses a mixture of carragheen moss (seaweed) and water as the base with special marbling inks floated on top. The second method is a demanding and complicated process requiring time and patience, but it yields more intricate and interesting patterns.

Marbling with oil paints is easy to set up and fun to do if you don't mind a bit of mess – children always enjoy it. The moss and inks method, on the other hand, is not suitable for children because the inks are toxic if swallowed even in minute quantities. Special care should be taken to wash hands before eating and drinking.

Carragheen moss can be obtained in its natural state or as a dry concentrated dust. The powder can be mixed with boiling water directly in the marbling tray. The seaweed should be placed in a saucepan of water (approximately a handful to half a pint of water), heated until boiling point, simmered for half an hour, left overnight, and then strained through a fine strainer. It should

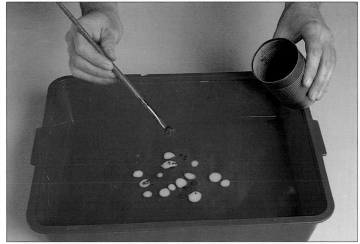

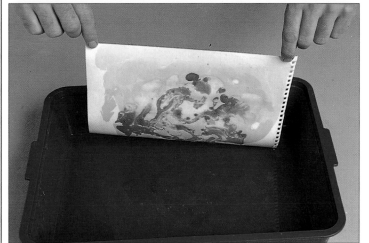

Oil paint marbling

1 The tank is prepared with hot water and gelatin, using a little more water than you would for making jam. If the mixture starts to gel, add more hot water. If you are using several colors, mix them separately, diluted with mineral spirits. When the colors are sprinkled onto the surface of the gelatin mixture, they should float; if they do not, add more mineral spirits or a little linseed oil – not too much, or it will leave marks on the paper.

2 Combs and other tools can be used to make patterns in the paint. Here a pointed awl is used to swirl it around. The thinner the paint, the more easily will it move around.

3 When you have made the pattern, take a piece of paper and carefully place it on the surface of the tank so that it lies flat, then remove it and wash off the excess gelatin under cold running water. Place the wet papers in between sheets of blotting paper and put some heavy weights on top so that the paper dries flat.

resemble soft jelly.

The inks are concentrated and need to be diluted with ox gall (available from art suppliers). An exact quantity cannot be given; the only way to know whether you have the right consistency is by experimenting. A drop of color floated on the seaweed mixture should expand to about 2 in (5 cm) in diameter. If it sinks or is too small, more ox gall is required, or you may need to adjust the seaweed mixture by diluting it with a little more hot water or adding more seaweed.

Once the colors float freely on the tank in circles without mixing together, they can be manipulated using combs and other implements.

To take a print, you must first treat the paper with alum water, which reduces the glue content and allows the inks to adhere. Mix two tablespoons of alum powder to one pint of hot water, sponge it onto the paper, and leave it to dry for a few minutes. The paper should be used just after it has dried; if it is too dry or too wet, you will not get a good print.

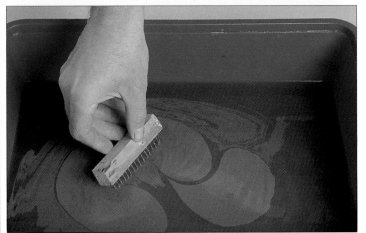

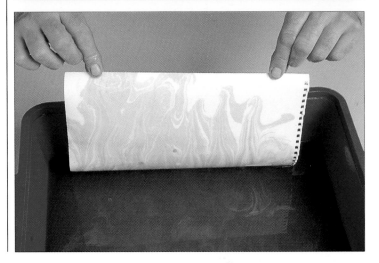

Seaweed and inks

1 The tank has been prepared with carragheen moss and water mixed to the consistency of thin jelly. This can be thinned further with hot water if necessary. When the colors are dropped onto the surface, they should float and expand to 2in (5cm) or more.

2 A variety of implements can be bought or improvised for marbling. Here a comb has been made with thin pins and a piece of wood. The special marbling inks can be maneuvered in more subtle ways than oil paints, and many intricate patterns can be made. For decorative papers to be used on mats or frames, you want to aim at a repeating effect as opposed to a totally random pattern, which can be achieved by repeating the movements you make as you manipulate the colors.

3 Before taking a print, wet the paper with alum water, allow it to dry a little but not completely, and then gently place it on top of the inks. Lift the paper and wash it under cold running water to remove excess seaweed, and dry it as for the oil-paint method. Clean the tank between prints by dragging some strips of newspaper across the surface.

Marbled inner mount

Marbled paper is best used in small quantities, or it can be overpowering. Here the paper has been folded over a deep bevel, which emphasizes the intense patterning. Although the paper is brightly colored, the visible margin is thin enough to prevent it from dominating the picture.

Marbled-paper borders

The marbled paper can also be cut into thin strips and glued onto a mat in place of a wash line. The paper strips should be mitered at the corners for a neater fit. This type of decoration is quite strong and is often used with prints of flowers and fruit, and other decorative images.

▶ If you do not have the time and patience to make marbled paper, a large variety of both machine-marbled and hand-marbled papers is available from specialist suppliers. These examples are hand made.

FABRIC MATS

Fabric mounts are often used for textiles and embroideries so that there is a physical consistency between the mount and the image. They can also look effective on drawings and paintings. Indian and Persian miniatures were traditionally mounted onto precious silks, with the fine fabric seeming to emphasize the jewel-like quality of the paintings themselves.

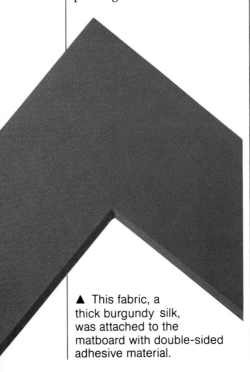

▲ This fabric, a thick burgundy silk, was attached to the matboard with double-sided adhesive material.

You can obtain fabric-covered matboards in a variety of colors and thicknesses, but they will, of course, be plain in the bevels of the windows. If you do not like this effect or cannot find a suitable fabric among the manufactured matboards, you can cover plain matboard with a fabric of your own choice. Some coarser fabrics such as burlap are sometimes painted after they have been attached to the board with a color chosen to complement the picture. This also slightly reduces the texture.

Fabric can be attached to the board in a number of ways. One is to use dry-mounting tissue, available from photographic suppliers. This is first attached to the board and then the fabric is ironed on. The advantage of this tissue is that it allows you to re-position the fabric if necessary by remelting the glue with the iron. Other suitable glues are latex-based fabric glues and spray-on mounting glues used by graphic designers. Some of the latter also allow for some re-positioning, but read the instructions carefully before you begin.

If you want to emphasize the bevel in a fabric mat, use a double-thickness board or glue two pieces of matboard together. Great care must be taken to smooth the material so that there are no creases, and to overlap corners and bevels neatly. To prevent any warping of the board as the glue is drying, it is a wise precaution to cover the fabric mat with another board and place some weights on top.

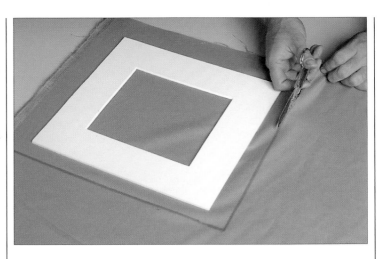

1 The window in the matboard is cut first. In this example, a thick board is used to accentuate the bevels, and the fabric is a thick gray velvet. Place the fabric below the mat, right side down, so that the marks will be on the reverse side, and cut it around the matboard, leaving a generous margin.

2 Place the fabric right side down on the mat and mark the dimensions of the window with a soft pencil. Cut out the central piece of fabric with a craft knife. Again, allow a generous margin, so that the fabric can be taken over the bevels.

3 Mark and then cut 45° miters in each corner of the fabric. Great care must be taken to make these accurate; a little too much and a gap will show and spoil the finish. Before gluing the fabric to the board, it must be ironed to remove all creases.

6 The mat is then placed upside down on the wrong side of the fabric. They are aligned carefully, and the fabric is turned over the bevels and ironed at a low heat. This melts the tissue, so that fabric and board stick together.

4 Thick fabrics can be glued on with latex, but in this case dry-mounting tissue was used. This leaves no marks on the fabric and allows for re-positioning if necessary. Here it is lightly tacked onto the front surface of the mat using an iron on a low heat.

5 Next the mat is turned upside down, and the flaps of dry-mounting tissue are ironed onto the back of the mat. This guarantees that the fabric will adhere to the bevels.

7 Finally, the mat is turned over to the right side, the alignment checked again, and the iron applied to attach the top surface to the mat. A fabric like this velvet could be damaged by heat, so it is protected with a piece of paper.

SPECIAL FINISHES

If you are in any doubt about the presentation of a picture, it is always safer to use neutral colors and minimal decoration. However, bolder and more unusual presentations can look effective for some images. The finishes discussed here are stronger than the traditional wash and pen lines*, but do not, of course, have to be used over the entire surface.

Texture

Gesso* can be used to create texture on mounts, stippled for a light texture, or for a heavier one, combed or painted on in patterns or lines. It is important to size the matboard with a little glue first and leave it to dry before applying the gesso.

Put on four or five coats, waiting only a short time between coats. The glossy wetness should have gone, but the gesso should still be damp as you apply the next coat. When you have the required depth of gesso, wait a few minutes for it to set before patterning. You will have to work fairly fast, but if the gesso becomes firm before you have finished, apply a further coat and try again.

There is a tendency for the board to warp if too much moisture is applied, so you may find it more satisfactory to use thicker board or particle board. In any case, it is advisable to weight the board while it is drying.

Gilding

Gold mounts were popular in the late Victorian era, but are less so today. A gold mount is now regarded as too overpowering for most pictures, but a small margin of gold can look very effective, particularly with some decorative images. For example, the inner margin of a double or triple mat* can be gilded so that only a small margin of gold is visible.

The easiest way to gild onto board is to use a water- or oil-based gold size to stick down transfer leaf* or imitation gold*. It is important to size the mat first to make the surface less absorbent. The best effects are obtained by laying one or two coats of burnishing clay under the gold, as in water gilding*, so that any faults will not expose the mat color, but give the appearance of old gold.

Laying imitation gold
1 First paint on water-based gold sizing, making sure that the brushmarks are blended into a smooth surface. In this case the bevel is to be gilded as well, so a window has been cut first.

2 After fifteen minutes, the sizing will be dry enough for the gold leaf to be applied. This is imitation gold which, unlike real gold leaf, can be picked up with the fingers and cut to size with scissors.

3 Apply the second leaf next to the first, and work methodically around the mat. The leaf will only stick where there is some glue.

4 Smooth down each piece of leaf with tissue paper taken from the book of leaf. To prevent tarnishing, the leaf must be lacquered.

BROKEN COLOR EFFECTS

Water-based colors sponged onto the surface of the mount can look effective, but care must be taken not to put too much water onto the board, as this can cause warping, and also the top paper, which is only glued down, may start to cockle and lift.

Several colors can be used, or you can restrict yourself to one and use the board itself as a second color. Paint can also be spattered and sprayed onto the mount surface, and you can achieve a wide variety of effects. Spraying with an airbrush will produce a delicate color wash formed by an almost imperceptible screen of colored dots, while for a slightly bolder effect, watercolor can be flicked on with a toothbrush or an artist's bristle brush.

Spattering is a messy process, so if you only want a margin of spattered color, you will have to mask the areas to be kept clean. Most adhesive tapes tend to damage matboard, so the best way to mask the mat is to cut a window in a piece of matboard the same length and width as the margin you wish to spatter.

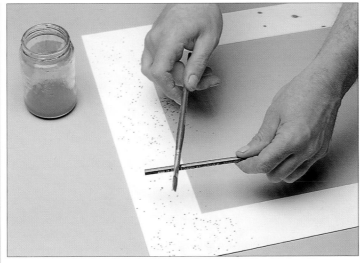

Spattering
1 Some crimson gouache paint was mixed as the first color. The paint needs to be well diluted with water so that the drops of color fall easily from the brush as it is knocked against the stick.

2 Blue gouache paint was then spattered over the red. Both brilliant and subtle colors can be achieved this way, with the color of the matboard contributing to the overall effect.

Sponging
1 Again, water-based paint is used, mixed with a little glue to give it more body.

2 Water is dropped onto the surface of the color to keep it moist.

3 While still wet, the color is sponged again to increase the density of the pattern.

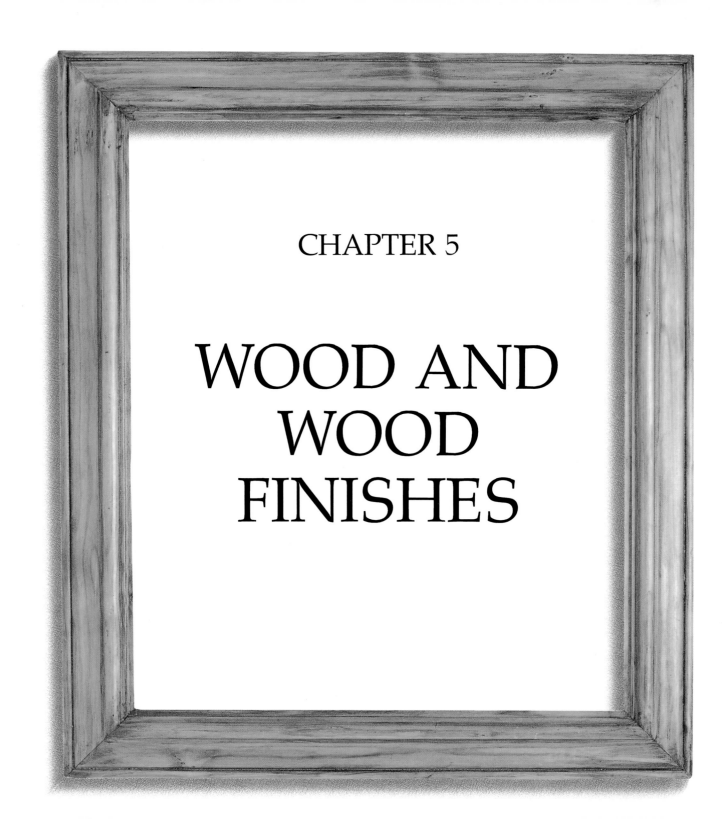

CHAPTER 5

WOOD AND WOOD FINISHES

There are a great many attractive woods, most of which are suitable for picture framing, but unfortunately you will find only a small selection are in ready-made molding form. A good reason for investing in a router or combination plane is that you can make original molding designs with any wood that is available. Those most commonly used by framemakers are listed on the next page, but there are other indigenous woods, which vary from country to country, such as fruitwoods, which are equally suitable for frames. There is also the possibility of using veneers; some of the rarer woods, and those with particularly attractive grains and patterns, are only available in veneer form.

Endangered woods

Nowadays there are ecological considerations involved in the choice of wood. The more widely available woods such as pine, ash, and oak are generally considered to come from sustainable forests in Europe and North America and are thus ecologically sound, but other popular woods, among them ramin, obeche, and mahogany, come from forests in Southeast Asia, Africa, and South America, which are not usually sustainable. Unfortunately, these tropical hardwoods are used extensively in the manufacture of frames and moldings, which makes it difficult to avoid them – many moldings are only available in these hardwoods. It is to be hoped, however, that refusing to buy these woods will eventually persuade the manufacturers to cease importing them.

VARIETIES OF WOOD

The woods most commonly used by professional picture framers are pine, ash, oak, ramin, obeche, and mahogany. Pine is a soft wood and is more prone to shrinkage and general damage than the hardwoods. It has a clearly defined grain, and poorer-quality pine is often studded with knots. However, it is cheap, widely available, and easy to cut, and is thus much used for framemaking. The surface is usually stained* or painted* to disguise the paleness of the wood, though it does not have to be.

Ash and oak are both durable hardwoods and are quite similar, though oak is usually darker. Both have attractive grains which make them ideal for frames with a natural wood finish, but they are also suitable for staining, oiling, pickling*, and painting. They are more expensive than some other hardwoods and almost twice the price of pine.

Ramin comes from Southeast Asia and is probably the most frequently used hardwood in picture framing at the present time. It has a pale, creamy brown color and a very close, even grain. This and its hardness allows moldings to be cut more finely than they can in soft pine, so it is often used for the more detailed design profiles.

Obeche comes from West Africa and is a soft, light, and somewhat featureless wood rather similar to balsa wood. Because of its lightness, it is useful for making wide-sectioned moldings. Mahogany, most of which comes from Brazil, is medium textured with a straight grain and a reddish-brown color. It is softer than most hardwoods and has an attractive finish.

*FURTHER INFORMATION

Wood stains	page 76
Paint finishes	pages 82-107
Pickling	page 74

◄ Wood veneers
Veneers are useful for natural wood finishes where you want a more exotic look than standard pine, oak, or ramin. They can only be used on flat or gently curved moldings, however.
1 Castello
2 Bird's eye maple
3 European walnut
4 Plane
5 Rosewood
6 Ash

▼ The russet colors of the fox and winter woodland are picked up in the rich-colored burr veneer molding. The print, "Red Fox," is by Carl Brenders, and the frame by Stephen and Linda Hible of Right Angle Picture Framing.

▲ These two frames were made by Stephen Field for portrait photographs. They are veneered in amboyna with boxwood lines (left) and yew with rosewood lines (right), and both are decorated with elegant fan inlays.

► There are many native European soft and hardwoods which can be used for making frames and furniture. They range in color and pattern from the pale sycamore and ash to the more colorful yew and fruitwoods.

1 Sycamore
2 Ash
3 Oak
4 Ash
5 Beech
6 Acacia
7 Pine
8 Cherry
9 Yew

PICKLING

Pickled wood, popular in the 1920s and 30s, is now enjoying a revival. It involves "pushing" white pigment into the wood grain, which gives a subtle emphasis to the pattern of the wood. Ash or oak are the woods most often chosen for this treatment, as their grain holds the white pigment well.

The grain can be made deeper by lightly scorching the surface, which burns out the softer wood to provide a deeper relief. This method is only suitable for ash and oak. Mature pine has a raised grain – you can often see it on old floorboards. To deepen the grain of new pine artificially, the wood must first be softened by wrapping wet rags around it and leaving for a day or overnight. The wood can then be scratched with a steel brush, leaving score marks which follow the grain of the wood.

For the pickling process itself, you can use either gesso* or pickling wax. Gesso can be made more intensely white by adding titanium white pigment to the mixture. Pickling wax can be bought ready made, but can also be mixed by adding titanium white to clear wax.

If gesso is used, warm it before application, and apply one or two coats with a brush so that all the grain is covered. When it is dry, wipe off the excess with a damp cloth.

With pickling wax, it is advisable to seal the wood first with a thin coat of shellac. When the shellac is dry, rub the pickling wax into the wood with fine steel wool to fill the grain, then rub on some clear wax to remove the excess white, and finally polish with a soft clean cloth.

Pickling wax is rather more difficult to rub off than gesso and tends to leave a white bloom over the whole surface of the wood. This residue can look attractive with certain pictures, but it can be removed with mineral spirits.

✱ FURTHER INFORMATION

Recipe for gesso   page 111

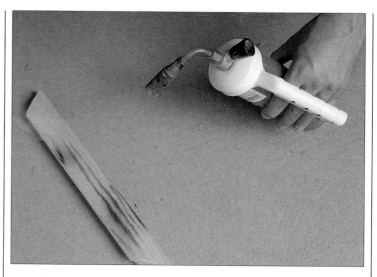

Scorching
A flat profile in oak is scorched using a plumber's blowtorch. Sweep the flame to and fro over each piece of the frame, being careful not to concentrate on any one area for too long. The rabbet, being the thinnest part of the frame, is particularly vulnerable to burning.

Pickling over scorched wood
Pickling wax is rubbed in with 0000 steel wool, which forces the white wax deep into the grain. The excess white wax is then cleaned off using either clear wax or mineral spirits. Here the pickled wood is seen next to a plain one. On the pickled section you can see the darker burned wood as well as the pickled grain.

Pickling plain wood

1 For a paler effect, simply rub pickling wax onto plain wood, allow it to dry, and then rub in some clear wax, which will take off most of the excess.

2 In this method of pickling a bloom of white is left over the whole surface. This can look attractive, but if not wanted it can be removed using mineral spirits.

Pickling with gesso

The traditional method of pickling is to paint gesso onto wood, usually oak or ash. For greater contrast, titanium white pigment can be added to the gesso mixture. One or two coats are usually enough to fill the grain. Allow the gesso to dry, and then wipe with a damp cloth or sponge, which helps to dissolve the glue in the gesso. The wood grain will be white, but the rest of the wood will be clean.

▶ These four samples show how the three pickling methods differ. The plain oak is shown at the bottom, with the gesso over scorched wood above it. Next is the plain wood with white wax, and at the top white wax over scorched wood. Pickling presents many possibilities, as you do not have to use white; other colors can be pushed into the grain.

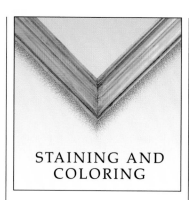

STAINING AND COLORING

In some cases a clear finish is suitable for a frame, but often a stain is used, either to complement a color in the picture or to enhance the natural grain and color of the wood. Before staining, the frame must be clean and should be sanded down to a smooth finish.

There are three types of wood stain: oil, alcohol, and water-based. Oil-based stains, available ready mixed in a wide choice of colors from most paint stores, are easy to apply and can be thinned – or removed completely – with mineral spirits.

Alcohol-based stains are aniline dyes which can be bought in powder form from specialist suppliers and mixed with denatured alcohol. There is a large range of colors available, including bright primaries, and they can be mixed together to obtain the exact shade you want. Denatured alcohol evaporates quickly, which can result in uneven coloring, but this can be remedied by rubbing with steel wool and a little denatured alcohol until an even spread of color is achieved. The powders can also be added to shellac* to make a colored French polish.

Water stains are also aniline dyes, but in this case they are, of course, water-soluble. They are available either in powder form or ready mixed, are easy to apply, and can be thinned with water.

All stains can be applied with either a brush or a rag, and the edges of the stain should be blended as quickly as possible. Protective gloves should be worn when applying wood stain.

✽**FURTHER INFORMATION**

Shellac, see under Waxes
   and polishes   page 81

▲ Spirit stains
These aniline dye stains are very concentrated, so they need to be mixed with a lot of denatured alcohol. Mix the stain thoroughly and test the color on the back of the frame or a spare piece of wood before applying it. The stain can either be brushed on or rubbed on with a cloth. If you rub it in, use protective gloves, as it is difficult to wipe off hands.

◄ Water stains
These are the same as spirit stains, except that the dyes are mixed with water rather than alcohol. There is a tendency for the water to lift the grain of the wood slightly, but when dry the frame can be rubbed smooth and then varnished and waxed.

▲ These have been colored with either water or spirit stains. Interesting color variations can be obtained by mixing and diluting the stains. The colors separate in a similar way to ink as they are diluted; for example, the black spirit stain turns an attractive purple-gray when thinned with denatured alcohol. Water and spirit stains are not compatible with one another and do not mix well with mineral color pigments.

— **Water-based stain (dye)**

— **Water-based stain**

— **Spirit stain**

— **Dye powder**

— **Dye powder**

— **Dye powder**

— **Shellac**

FUMED WOOD

Fuming is a process of coloring wood by exposing it to the fumes of ammonia. The depth of color can be controlled by the length of exposure.

You will need an airtight "fume tent," which you can make by covering a light wooden frame with black plastic and sealing the joints of the plastic with tape. When using ammonia, wear goggles and a face mask. Put the frame inside the tent with some saucers containing ammonia, leave for a day, and then check the color. If a darker color is required, leave the frame in the tent, checking from time to time.

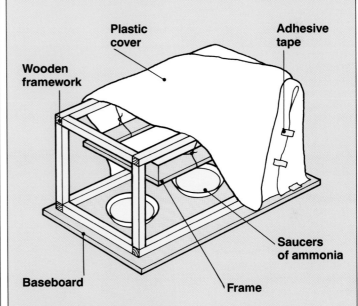

Plastic cover

Adhesive tape

Wooden framework

Saucers of ammonia

Baseboard

Frame

▶ These two corners of oak molding show the difference between the natural wood and the fumed wood, which in this case was left in a fume cupboard with a saucer of strong ammonia for twenty-four hours. Diluted household ammonia can be used, but will take much longer to color the wood.

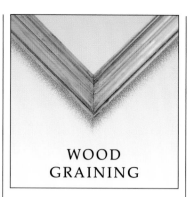

WOOD GRAINING

Imitation wood graining is a method which has been practiced for many years. It was particularly popular in the Victorian era, when pine furniture and the trim of urban houses were made to look like oak.

The most widely used method of wood graining is to use an oil-and-driers medium known as a scumble glaze* over a biscuit-colored undercoat or, for exotic finishes such as ebony, maple, satinwood, and tulipwood, a smooth gesso undercoat. Scumble glazes are available from fine-art suppliers or decorative-paint stores, either in their basic transparent form or ready mixed in a wide range of wood colors. For a special color, you can mix your own using artist's oil colors.

A wide selection of tools and brushes has been devised for the graining itself. These include steel and rubber combs and rockers for simulating the pattern of wood graining and blending brushes for brush graining; stippling brushes and feathers for backgrounds.

When attempting any imitation effect, whether wood grain or precious stone, it is essential to have adequate visual reference, either a small sample of the actual material, or a good photograph. If you try to work from memory, you will almost certainly make the pattern too repetitive; in nature, there is always a subtle non-conformity.

The fascination of rare and exotic woods lies in their depth of color, patterns, and smooth surface, and to simulate these effects in paint, it is essential to keep the surface equally smooth and even. This is done by keeping the paint film to a minimum and rubbing with fine abrasives when the paint is dry.

✱FURTHER INFORMATION

Paints, mediums,
  and varnishes   page 86

2 The frame has been gessoed, smoothed down, and then painted with an ocher shellac undercoat. The first oil colors are now stippled on. The colors used are raw umber, burnt umber, raw sienna, and burnt sienna.

1 The paints used for the first stage are oil colors. Here a scumble glaze, which keeps the paints wet and easy to manipulate, is mixed with liquid driers and mineral spirits to speed up the drying time.

3 The brush is charged with glaze before some color is picked up (burnt and raw umber) and dabbed onto the frame in a deliberately haphazard way. The two sienna colors are applied in the same way, and the process is repeated.

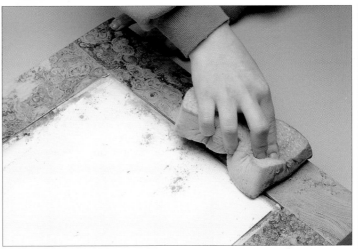

4 To simulate the effect of a butt joint, a piece of sandpaper is used face down as a barrier, and excess color is wiped off one side of the frame. The sandpaper will not smudge the wet oil color.

7 The Fuller's earth is then wiped off with a sponge and water. In this picture you can see the effect of the simulated butt joint very clearly. This is the traditional way of joining wood veneer.

5 The wood grain effect is built up slowly and gradually, with cotton swabs, old pencils, and brushes used to take off and add color in a circular motion. At this stage, the color is left to dry overnight.

6 When the oil color is dry, Fuller's earth (or finely ground chalk) is sprinkled onto the surface. This process, known as "cissing," reduces the oil and helps the top colors to adhere.

8 The top color now being used is water-based, and so it is necessary to make a binder, or it will not adhere to the lower layer of oil. In this case one part vinegar to three parts water is used.

9 The water-based paint, crystals of Vandyke brown soaked overnight in water, is applied with a large brush charged with binder and color.

10 The same brush, a camel-hair "cutter" brush, is rocked and moved up and down to mottle and wave the surface.

11 Finally, the top color needs to be "strapped down" using an oil-based eggshell varnish, thinned with mineral spirits on the first coat. Wood graining is a slow process, but in this case has produced a marvelously convincing impression of burr walnut.

▶ **Walnut grain**
These samples, of a different type of walnut, were painted in the same way as the frame, starting with oil colors on top of an ocher undercoat. The distinctive grain markings were made by dragging a rubber rocker through the wet oil paint, and watercolor was later added to give more light to the pattern. The demonstration and the samples were done by Louise Taylor.

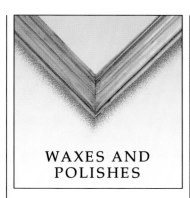

WAXES AND POLISHES

There are four main categories of finishes applied to raw wood: wax, shellac, lacquer and varnish, and oil.

Wax gives an attractive eggshell finish and is very simple to apply, requiring no equipment other than a rag. There are many types of wax polish, but the beeswax-based ones are most often used for wood. If you want to add a touch of color to pale wood, you can mix powder pigment with clear wax, or use one of the ready-mixed color waxes that correspond to different wood colors.

Shellac, a varnish made from the secretion of an insect (the lac), goes under many different names, including French polish and button polish. It is sold ready mixed in cans or as flakes which can be mixed in alcohol.

It can be applied either with a brush or with a French polishing pad, which is simply a square of linen wrapped around a piece of cotton batting which has first been soaked with shellac. A little linseed oil is used as a lubricant.

If you apply shellac with a brush, you can put on several coats in a short time; a new coat can be applied as soon as the first is "touch-dry." You must leave it longer than this before sanding, however – a minimum of two hours – as it will still be tacky underneath.

Shellac is a versatile finish and can be mixed with aniline alcohol dyes* and pigments to make colored finishes as well. Its only disadvantage is that it is not very water- or heat-resistant and so should not be used for frames to be hung in a bathroom or kitchen.

Nitrocellulose lacquers and varnishes are very hard, moisture-proof, and heat-resistant. They are also very quick drying and when used industrially are usually applied with a spray-gun, though a brush can also be used. Precatalyzed plastic lacquers have similar characteristics. They will give a durable high-gloss finish. Make sure that they are compatible with any paints or stains underneath. They react badly to oily surfaces.

Modern wood varnishes such as polyurethane* are also extremely hard-wearing and water- and heat-resistant. They take twelve hours or more to dry, and should be sanded between coats.

Oils, usually Danish oil and tung oil, are traditionally used on oily woods such as teak which resist other finishes, but they can also be used effectively on other hardwoods and softwoods. Oil nourishes and protects wood, and leaves an attractive natural appearance. You will need to apply three or four coats, allowing six hours' drying time between the first two coats and twenty-four hours for any subsequent ones.

*FURTHER INFORMATION

Wood stains	page 78
Paints, mediums, and varnishes	page 86

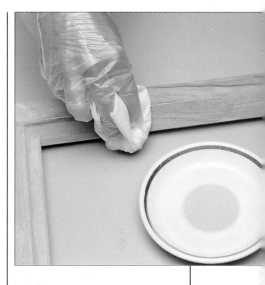

Shellac
Here shellac is applied with a homemade version of the French-polishing pad. This is simply a pad of cotton batting dipped in shellac and wrapped in a rag.

Wax
Wax is quickly and easily applied with a rag. Progressive applications over a period of time will build up a rich glow without substantially changing the color of the wood.

Oil
Danish oil imparts a rich golden color. If the grain becomes raised and rough when using either oil or shellac, rub with steel wool between coats.

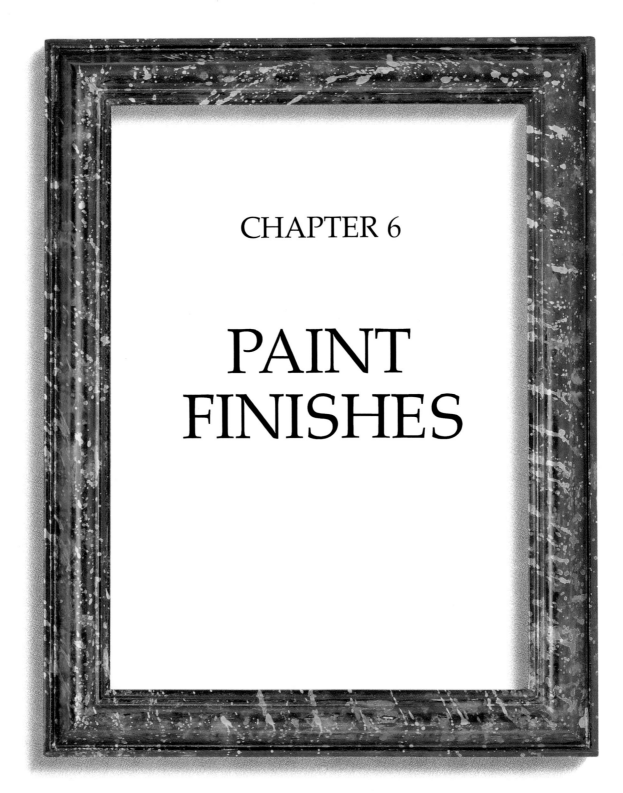

CHAPTER 6

PAINT FINISHES

An ever-increasing range of predecorated picture frame moldings is available today, with many elaborate and attractive finishes in both modern and traditional designs. You may find that your requirements are adequately catered to by molding manufacturers, but many people still prefer hand-finished frames, with shapes, colors, and textures chosen for individual pictures.

The more delicate and refined finishes, such as water gilding and color washes over gesso, can seldom be supplied by molding manufacturers, mainly because these finishes are fragile and would require careful transporting and storage, as well as many layers of protective lacquer. The latter would in many cases destroy the effect, as the beauty of hand-finished frames often lies in their unvarnished surface and the original designs of the framer.

Decorative paint finishes are usually applied after the frame has been assembled, with the finish painted over the mitered corners to give a neater, more attractive appearance.

UNDERCOATING

Before applying a paint finish, absorbent surfaces are usually treated with some form of size. This can be animal-skin glue or white or yellow glue* thinned with a little water. Whichever you use, allow it to dry before applying paint. To achieve a smooth top surface, the next step is to put some undercoats onto the frame, thus forming a good base to hold the subsequent layers of paint.

Ordinary latex or oil paint can be used as undercoats as long as they are compatible with the paint that is to be used on top.

Gesso*, important in the gilding process, is also used as an undercoat for painted finishes. It is normally made from whiting and rabbit-skin glue, but can also be made with casein (see recipe). The advantage of casein gesso is that it can be stored and used cold, unlike skin-glue gesso which has to be heated.

*FURTHER INFORMATION

Paints, mediums and varnishes	page 86
Recipe for gesso	page 111

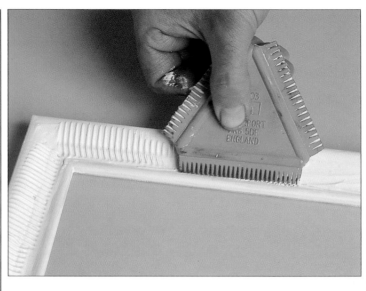

Texture
1 Some paint finishes are improved by an underlying texture. You can make a variety of raised patterns in thick gesso or wet plaster by combing, stippling, or pressing a rough fabric into the surface.

Preparation
To prime the wood and provide a smooth, well-sealed surface for a paint finish, you can use household oil undercoats, latex paint, or acrylic gesso, depending on the type of paint to be used on top.

2 Here a thin wash of water-based paint is applied over the combed-gesso texture.

3 A damp sponge is lightly drawn over the surface, removing some of the paint from the ridges to highlight the effect.

4 The first color has been allowed to dry, and a darker one laid on top. The finished frame can be seen on page 162.

RECIPE FOR CASEIN SIZE AND GESSO

Ingredients
- Powdered casein 2 parts
- Water 16 parts
- Ammonium carbonate (powdered) 1 part
- Whiting

Method
Use fresh casein if possible, because it loses its strength with time. Mix it into half the water, stirring to get rid of any lumps.

For gesso, simply add enough whiting to the casein solution to make a creamy consistency. If it does not seem smooth, strain it through a fine strainer.

Add the ammonium carbonate, stir again, and leave to stand for one hour before adding the remaining water. This mixture can be used as a size or as a vehicle for paint or gesso.

To make paint, add finely ground pigments to the casein and a little water to thin if required.

PAINTS, MEDIUMS AND VARNISHES

Because there are so many types of paint and varnish available, this summary may provide a useful reference. Remember that it is important to handle paints and varnishes with care. The mineral pigments used in most paints are poisonous, and many of the solvents are highly toxic. Work in a well-ventilated room, avoid eating or drinking while you work, and wear protective clothing if you are using toxic substances. Gloves, goggles, and masks are available from most paint stores and home centers.

PAINTS

Types	Composition	Uses
Acrylic (artist's)	Finely ground pigments in water-soluble acrylic base	A strong solid flat-finish paint. When thinned, it is suitable for washes. Water-resistant when dry
Gouache and poster paint	Pigments mixed with gum arabic or synthetic compounds. Additional filler makes gouache more opaque than watercolor	A thick opaque watercolor with a flat matte finish
Oil color (artist's)	Pigments finely ground in oil, usually linseed or poppy	Comprehensive colour choice. Can be thinned for color washes and suspended in mediums for glazes. Strong color
Egg tempera	Finely ground pigment in an egg-yolk and water medium	An attractive paint for thin color washes, can also be used for denser color effects
Watercolor (artist's)	Finely ground pigments mixed with gum arabic and other binders	Good for translucent color washes and for tinting over gold and silver
Decorator's latex	Synthetic resins and pigments	Available in a wide choice of colors and finishes. It can be diluted for use as a wash. Also useful as an undercoat. Water-resistant when dry
Decorator's oil-based paint	Pigments and synthetic compounds	A thick, durable paint, available in many colors and finishes

MEDIUMS AND VARNISHES

Casein	Casein (substance made from the curd of milk). Bought in powder form and mixed with ammonium carbonate and water	Used as a glue, size, or as a medium to make a durable and thick paint with an attractive velvet flat-finish. Water-resistant when dry
PVA (Polyvinyl acetate)	Colorless resin used in latex paints and glues	A useful glue and, in thinned form, paint medium. Water-resistant when dry
Transparent oil glaze ("scumble")	Oil- and resin-based medium with driers	Very useful as a paint medium for marbling, woodgraining, and other paint finishes
Acrylic varnish	Acrylic resin in petroleum solvent (also water-based version)	Colorless varnish that dries to a satin finish
Polyurethane varnish	Synthetic resins and oil base	Widely available household varnish. Suitable for all decorative finishes, but tends to yellow with age
Shellac (french polish)	Insect deposits suspended in alcohol	Useful as a medium for color lacquers, as a varnish, and as an isolating layer between films of paint
Damar and mastic varnishes	Naturally occurring resins suspended in oil	Clear varnishes for oil-based paints. Long-lasting with good protective properties

Solvents	Drying time and peculiarities
Water	Touch dry in 5–10 minutes. Good covering power, but expensive for large areas
Water	Touch dry in a few minutes. A traditional thick watercolor, useful for precise paintwork. Good covering power
Turpentine or mineral spirits	Touch dry in 24 hours, but longer final drying time. Can be made to dry more quickly with alkyd and other driers. Useful for many paint effects
Water	Touch dry in a few minutes, but takes longer to dry fully. More difficult to use than some other water-based paints. Also used for sgraffito over gold
Water	Touch dry in a few minutes. Must be varnished or waxed, because it remains water-soluble when dry and is therefore vulnerable
Water	Quick drying decorator's paint (1–3 hours). Inexpensive and available at most home stores. Good covering power
Turpentine or mineral spirits	Slow drying (6–12 hours). More often used on large areas. Needs a primer and undercoat for an effective finish
Water	A form of gesso can be made with casein size. Good for building up layers of undercoat. Touch dry in 10–20 minutes
Water	Touch dry in approximately 20 minutes. Also useful as a size, sealer and varnish
Turpentine or mineral spirits	A flexible medium that allows manipulation with feathers, combs and rags for 30 minutes. Dry in approximately 6 hours
Water	Touch dry in approximately 1 hour. Easy to use, an all purpose decorator's varnish
Turpentine or mineral spirits	Dry in 6–12 hours. A tough varnish available in matt, silk and gloss finishes
Denatured alcohol	Touch dry in 5–10 minutes, but must not be rubbed down for 2 hours after application
Turpentine or mineral spirits	Slow drying time: approximately 24 hours. An attractive gloss finish

COLOR WASHES

Although there are so many different types of paint, they can be divided into two broad categories – transparent and opaque. A thin paint lying over a lighter ground will appear transparent because light is reflected back through the top layer from the light background. When, on the other hand, the coat of paint lies on a background of the same color or a darker one, the background does not reflect light, and the effect is called "opaque."

Laying transparent color washes, either with oil or watercolor paints, is a technique which has been practiced by artists and decorators for centuries. For maximum luminosity, a white ground is used, which could be either white paint or gesso. The system of painting one color over another creates greater variations of depth of tone than one single coat and can produce very beautiful color harmonies.

Color lacquers, similarly, are usually built up layer by layer on a smooth ground – the more layers you use, the less transparent the effect.

Lacquers can be made by putting dry pigment or aniline dyes* into shellac*, which dries very quickly – in five to ten minutes – allowing you to build up several layers in a short time. However, even when "touch-dry," the shellac will still remain tacky underneath, so allow two hours' drying time before rubbing. If you want a high gloss, rub only every two or three coats and the penultimate one with a light abrasive such as "wet-and-dry" sandpaper or 0000 steel wool. For an eggshell finish, you can use the same abrasives, but rub each coat before the final one, and for a flat finish, the last coat can also be rubbed down.

✳FURTHER INFORMATION

Waxes and polishes   page 81

1 Before a color wash is applied, the frame should be prepared with gesso and sanded to a smooth finish. The gesso is then given a coat of rabbit-skin sizing to make it less absorbent and insure an even spread of color. With the sizing now dry, the first color, an indigo blue, is painted onto the central margin.

2 The next color, a mixture of burnt sienna and yellow ocher, is painted onto the sides and outer edge. Choose a brush of appropriate shape and size for the area being painted, so that it can be easily brushed along the margin. If a darker shade is required, another coat can be applied as soon as the first one has dried.

3 To soften or remove the colors in places, wipe a damp sponge around the frame, which will also even out any overlapping brushstrokes. Here the sponge is used to remove color from the high outside edge, emphasizing the molding profile.

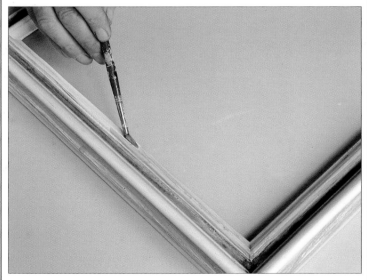

4 Finally, a mixture of yellow and yellow ocher is painted onto the sight edge margin to echo the color of the outside edge. Many color combinations can be tried, chosen to harmonize with the picture, and modified with water for subtle variations.

▶ The light blue and brown used in the painting were repeated on the frame. Watercolor paints were used, protected with a layer of clear wax.

▶ Bright colors were painted onto a gesso ground with watercolor and then washed off the ridges. When dry, the frame was waxed with a dark brown wax to soften the colors.

DISTRESSED PAINT EFFECTS

The passage of time and the general effects of wear and tear give a mature and subtle patina to old painted frames, and this aging is often simulated on new ones to impart a richer color and softer appearance.

Distressing a paint surface is done by rubbing off some of the top layer of paint, thus exposing the undercoat, something which occurs naturally with age. Oriental laquerware (*Negoro nuri*), for example, was first lacquered in black and then in red. As the top layer was repeatedly polished, the black undercoat began to show through, enhancing the rich appearance.

First apply two or three coats of undercolor. The underpainting must be strong enough to remain undamaged when abrasives are applied to the top coat. This top layer needs to be densely colored, but not too thick, as it is obviously easier to rub off a thin coat of paint.

All the paint must be dry before rubbing, or the abrasives will stick and leave unsightly furrows in the surface. Either water- or oil-based paints can be used, or they can be combined, in which case the water-based color must lie beneath the oil.

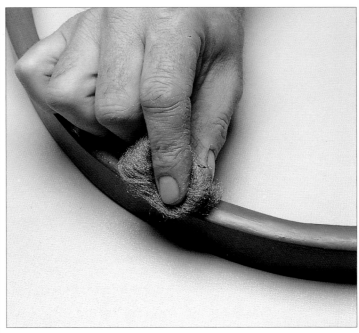

Water-based paint
1 Ordinary latex paint or artist's acrylics can be used for the first coat. Here two coats of red latex have been applied over a surface prepared with gesso. When dry, a coat of green was applied on top, allowed to dry in turn, and then lightly rubbed with steel wool.

2 Fine sandpaper, which is more abrasive than steel wool, is now used to remove more of the green top coat. Care must be taken not to rub too hard or to use too coarse a grade of sandpaper, or the lower layer of paint will also begin to come off.

Burnishing clay

1 A terracotta burnishing clay over a gesso ground was used as an undercoat, and to make this thick and strong, three coats were painted on. When the top coat is distressed by rubbing with an abrasive, the undercoat must remain solid. The top coat in this case is black clay, applied over the red base coat.

2 When the top coat is dry, it can be rubbed with either 0000 steel wool or a fine wet-and-dry abrasive sandpaper, which will partially remove the black to reveal the red beneath. Other types of paint can be distressed in a similar manner, sometimes using a solvent as well as an abrasive for the top coat.

▶ The base coat was an ocher latex, protected with an acrylic varnish. The top coat, a dark purple latex, was rubbed through very thoroughly so that both colors feature equally strongly.

▶ A black undercoat of casein-based paint was first protected with an acrylic varnish and then covered with a thin top coat of green acrylic and distressed with fine abrasives.

CRACKLE FINISHES

In principle, putting a slow-drying paint or varnish below a faster-drying one should be avoided. Paint or varnish shrinks slightly as it dries, and as the slow-drying lower layer contracts, it will cause cracks in the dry upper one. However, these small cracks on a surface can be attractive and are sometimes deliberately induced by applying a glaze of gum arabic and ox gall over an oil-based varnish.

The timing between the two coats is critical, as by varying the drying times you can control the size of the cracks. They will in any case be very fine, so the effect is usually emphasized by rubbing in a color, usually an oil paint.

Another type of crackle agent is a transparent water-based glaze called Pervolac, produced for the film industry to create instant cracked-paint effects. To be effective, Pervolac needs to be sandwiched between two layers of latex or other water-based paints. For this type of crackle glaze, it is best to apply the top coat of latex paint with an airbrush rather than a bristle brush, which can cause furrows in the soft glaze.

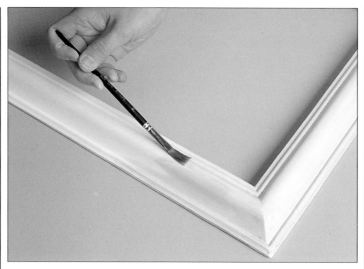

Varnish crackle
1 The paint or gesso surface should be rubbed smooth before the application of the crackle glazes. Here gesso is used as a base coat and has been sealed to make it less absorbent. You can use either sizing or shellac varnish. The oil-based varnish, with added color for an aging effect, is then painted evenly over the surface.

2 The water-based varnish is painted on top when the oil varnish is still moist, but not tacky. The brand used here, called Crackleur, needs twenty to thirty minutes. The length of time between each application determines the extent of the crackling. You may need to experiment, as varnishes react to atmospheric conditions.

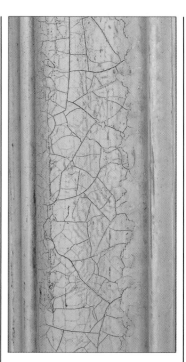

3 To emphasize the cracks, which are practically invisible on their own, a little umber oil paint has been rubbed over the frame. The underlying varnish takes some time to dry and cause the cracking. This could be anything from a few hours to a few days, depending on atmospheric conditions and the thickness of the lower layer of varnish.

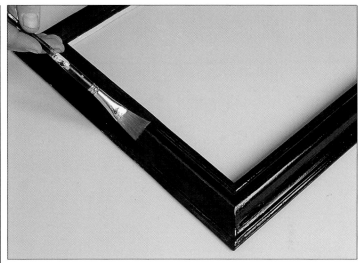

4 The water-based top glaze is vulnerable to damp, so it is wise to protect the finish with a wax or a varnish. Wait until the oil paint or ink in the cracks is dry before applying the top protection.

Pervolac
1 Pervolac is a thick water-based glaze designed to be used with an airbrush, but it can also be applied with a soft paintbrush. Here it is painted over a black latex base coat. It is important to paint an even covering in order to achieve cracks of the same dimension.

USING GOLD

Many variations of color and paint can be tried for both the base coat and the cracks. In this example, varnish was painted on top of red burnishing clay, water glaze was applied on top, and gold wax was then rubbed into the cracks.

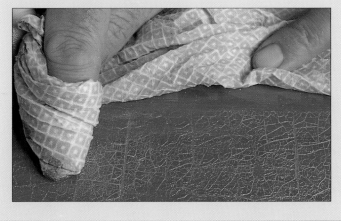

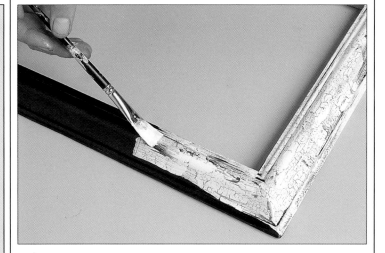

2 When the Pervolac has gelled, but not hardened (approximately ten to twenty minutes), apply the top coat of paint. In this case the top coat is white latex, chosen to create a dramatic black-crack effect. Be careful with brushstrokes on the top layer, because too much pressure will break the weak skin of the glaze.

Pervolac with an airbrush

1 Again, Pervolac was brushed over a black base coat, and yellow latex sprayed on top with an airbrush. Colors can be mixed with a suitable water medium such as acrylic, white glue, or latex paint, but must not be too thick or they will be difficult to spray. The latex is sprayed on with a back-and-forth motion to provide an even coating all over the frame. The top layer of paint begins to crack almost immediately.

▲ The frame was first coated with black oil paint, and then "crackleur" varnish was applied. This comes in two parts, an oil varnish, which is used first, and a water-based one; the action of the two forms the cracks.

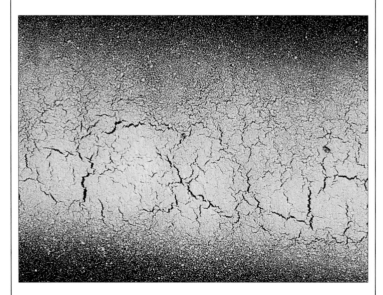

2 Different patterns of cracking can be achieved by varying the texture of the paint. Thicker paint will give broader cracks, while the thin, diluted latex used in this example gives close, delicate cracks. The airbrush also allows you to experiment with the drying time of the Pervolac glaze.

▶ In this case, dark red paint mixed with shellac was applied before the "crackleur" varnish. Pale green paint was rubbed in to emphasize the cracks; it appears almost white against the rich deep red.

EGGSHELL INLAY

An attractive and unusual surface can be created by gluing eggshells onto a ground and then grouting in the cracks. This gives a mosaic-like effect, which can be either painted, gilded, or left as a natural color and varnished.

The eggshells must first be soaked in a solution of household bleach (sodium hypochlorite), for at least two days. This breaks down the membranes of the shell and makes it easier to stick them onto the frame – as well as removing any residue of egg white. White glue is painted onto the surface of the frame, and the pieces of eggshell are pressed into place.

When the glue is dry, grout is rubbed between the cracks to create a smooth surface, after which the eggshell can be sanded with fine wet-and-dry sandpaper and varnished.

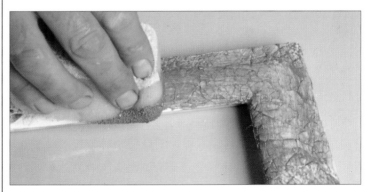

1 After bleaching for two days and rinsing in vinegar and water, the eggshells are ready to glue on. The frame should be smooth and sealed with a glue or a varnish. To glue the eggshell, simply apply white glue to a small part of the frame and press each one into place. Continue working section by section.

2 The long sides of the eggshell are easier to press because they are flatter than the more sharply curved top edges. Press the eggshell until it cracks and lies flat against the frame. It is obviously easier to do this over a flat or gently curved molding profile.

3 When all the spaces have been filled and the glue is dry, the cracks are filled in with grout. Commercial brands of floor- and wall-tile grout, which are available in both white and a range of colors, can be used. If you are unable to find a suitable color, you can mix white grout with dry pigments. Wipe all excess grout off the eggshell before it dries.

4 In this example, a dark gray grout was used as a contrast to the natural color of the eggshells. When the grout is dry, the whole surface can be rubbed smooth and then protected with coats of varnish, shellac, or wax. You can also use paint on top of the eggshells, or even gild the surface.

MARBLE AND LAPIS LAZULI

Painted imitation marble has a long history, and various ingenious methods of simulating its grain have been devised. Semiprecious stones such as lapis lazuli can also be imitated on frames.

Either water- or oil-based paints can be used for these finishes, but oil paint is easier to use, as its slow-drying quality allows more time to create the effect you want. A useful medium for all decorative work with oil paint is scumble glaze*, made with linseed oil and driers. When mixed with oil paint, the additional oil provides flexibility, while the driers cut down the drying time.

The background color may feature in the final surface, so it should be chosen carefully. It is important to begin with a firm undercoat and then protect it with shellac or varnish, which enables you to experiment with the top layers of paint without disturbing the base coat.

*FURTHER INFORMATION

Paints, mediums,
and varnishes   page 86

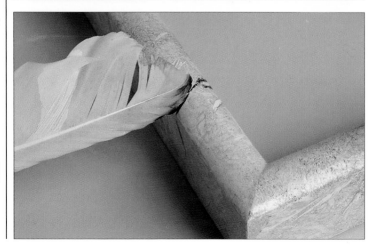

Marble

1 A fine smooth ground is essential for any imitation-stone finish. In this case, a gesso surface was rubbed smooth and sealed with rabbit-skin sizing. Artist's oil paints – ocher and burnt sienna – were mixed with scumble glaze and are now stippled onto the frame.

2 To make the background texture pattern, the paint is dabbed on with a rag. The film of paint is thin enough to allow the luminosity of the brilliant white gesso to show through. This finish simulates Sienese marble, in which some white is usually visible, and this effect is best achieved by exposing the white gesso in places.

3 Delicate patterning and subtle blends of color can be achieved with a feather dipped in mineral spirits. Here the feather is used as a brush to paint the black veins typical of this type of marble. Some white gesso is exposed within the veins. When the oil paint is dry, it can be lightly rubbed and then varnished or waxed for extra protection.

▲ This composite marble frame made by Isabella Kocum is reminiscent of table tops of marble and semiprecious gemstones made in Renaissance times. The individual shapes of the patterned stones were drawn and engraved on gesso.

▶ The distinctive gray and white markings of Sicilian marble have been imitated on the frame at the top. The finish was painted with scumble glaze mixed with oil paint, and the veining was done with a feather and blending brushes. The other frame (right), also marbled, has gilt corner ornaments in pastiglia (see page 120). The marbling was done in the same way, but in this case the white markings were achieved by exposing the gesso undercoat. Both frames were made by Isabella Kocum.

3 The colors should be wet with scumble glaze, so that they can be manipulated to form convincing patterns.

Lapis lazuli

1 The surface should be painted with gesso or undercoat and sanded smooth. Two or more black base coats are then applied, followed by a coat of shellac to protect the surface. Artist's oil paints, in ultramarine, cobalt, and cerulean blue are mixed separately with scumble glaze and brushed on in approximately the same quantities around the frame.

2 A stippling brush can be used to spread the color evenly. Rags or thin plastic bags are then pressed into the paint to provide a background pattern similar to crystalline stone.

4 Dropping or spraying mineral spirits or turpentine onto the paint surface makes the colors "float," and this floating film of paint can form interesting and intricate patterns as the solvent reveals patches of the black base color.

5 Marks made with a feather are much more delicate than any brushstroke. Goose feathers are the best for this purpose, as they are more robust than other types, and can be cleaned and re-used.

Sweeping strokes and a stippling motion can be tried with the feather. If necessary, more paint can be applied using the feather as a brush.

7 When you have achieved the blue-on-black patterns, sprinkle on some bronze powder in small quantities. Lapis lazuli has a characteristic gold fleck. The bronze powder will adhere to the wet oil paint.

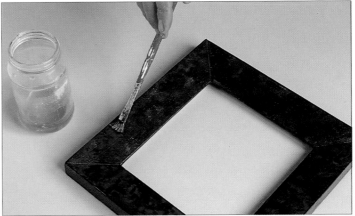

6 Make sure that there is little or no buildup of paint texture on the surface. Lapis lazuli and other semiprecious stones usually have highly polished surfaces which must be duplicated in the paint finish.

8 When the oil paint is fully dry (this could take several days), rub the surface with various grades of wet-and-dry sandpaper until a silky, smooth surface is obtained. This can then be varnished or waxed.

VERDIGRIS

This is the attractive blue-green patina that forms on copper, brass, and bronze; you see it most often on bronze-cast statuary.

It is a crystalline substance (hydrated copper acetate), which was used as a color pigment in antiquity, but proved unreliable. As a pigment, it is now obsolete, but you can create a similar color effect by using viridian (a dark bluish-green) as a background color. This can be bought in pigment form and mixed with glue (white or casein) or bought ready made as latex paint. You will need three additional colors, which can be mixed in a similar way: a pale blue, a pale green, and a small quantity of yellow ocher.

When the viridian undercoat is dry, stipple on some of the paler colors in a random manner around the frame, and then throw on plenty of water to expose some of the undercoat. Finally, dust some whiting or plaster over the surface so that it sticks to the paint. When dry, the surplus dust can be wiped off, and white glue or flat water-based finish applied to protect the surface.

2 With the light colors still wet, water was dropped onto the surface to reveal parts of the viridian undercoat, which will feature in the overall finish.

1 A dark green (viridian) latex paint was applied as a base coat, rubbed smooth, and protected with a layer of acrylic varnish. A light blue and a light green were then mixed with latex paint and stippled over the undercoat.

3 To create a textured, crumbly surface imitating that of real verdigris, whiting is sprinkled onto the wet paint.

4 The whiting is then dabbed with a rag to mix the powder into the paint. Be careful not to use too much whiting, or the paint film will become weak, and there will be a danger that it will flake off.

6 Finally, to imitate the intense green of verdigris, an oil glaze of viridian was painted all over the water paints, and a layer of flat acrylic varnish was applied.

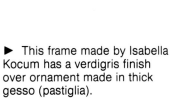

5 A water-based yellow ocher paint is spattered onto the surface by dragging a loaded brush across a stick to release small drops of color onto the painted surface.

▶ This frame made by Isabella Kocum has a verdigris finish over ornament made in thick gesso (pastiglia).

SPATTERING

Spattering is an elementary exercise in decoration, but unless you work methodically, you can get into a terrible mess. Take care to cover all areas around the frame, and also your eyes and face.

You can use various paints and methods, depending on the effect you want. Spattering methods include knocking a paintbrush against a block of wood to release small drops of paint; stroking a paint-loaded brush against a stick or a piece of window screen; and using a toothbrush instead of a paintbrush, draw your thumb across it to flick color at the frame.

Whichever method you use, you can create different types of pattern by varying the consistency of the paint and the distance between the spattering implement and the frame. You can also spatter solvents on a colored paint film, which can yield interesting effects.

*FURTHER INFORMATION

Paints, mediums,
and varnishes   page 86

Paint and solvent
1 The frame was given a black undercoat of casein paint, providing a background to contrast with the bright top colors. A thin mixture of shellac colors is now tapped onto the surface.

2 After spattering the surface with a selection of bright colors, denatured alcohol is dropped onto the paint. This separates the color and causes it to float, so that it can be manipulated more easily.

3 When the shellac and paint have dried, it is rubbed with 0000 steel wool to smooth the surface.

4 Finally the surface is protected with acrylic varnish. Be careful with the choice of varnish; some could act as a solvent on the spattered paint. Acrylic varnish is a safe choice.

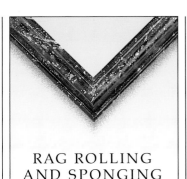

RAG ROLLING AND SPONGING

Rag rolling is a method of decoration often used on large areas such as walls, but it is equally effective on frames.

The best results are obtained by mixing oil paints with the transparent oil scumble glaze* mentioned earlier. This thins the paint and allows greater flexibility. The color is then stippled onto the frame and while still wet, a rolled rag – preferably one with some texture – is pushed in varying directions along it. The rag should be moistened with mineral spirits or turpentine so that it can move freely without sticking.

Rag rolling is also used to soften other painted effects such as marbling and can be used for the background texture as well.

A related method is sponging, in which the texture is provided by that of the sponge. You could try out different types of sponge, both synthetic and natural.

In this case, water-based colors can be used, mixed with wallpaper sizing, which stays wet for an hour or more to allow the sponge to be manipulated to create delicate patterns. This method can be used on paper or matboard as well, and is sometimes used for decorative mats.

Sponging

1 Black water-based casein paint is sponged onto a dry red undercoat. The gilded finish on each side of the painted margin is protected with a piece of cardboard. The natural sponge leaves an interesting texture, and while the paint is still wet, it can be dampened in clean water and pressed around the frame again to thin the top color.

▲ The rich appearance of the sponged black on red border is further amplified by the gilded sight edge and margin. The frame has been completed with a black lacquered outside edge.

Sponging

▶ A pale green background was painted on with latex paint. This was allowed to dry, and then white latex was sponged on top with a small natural sponge.

▶ This frame has an ocher latex undercoat and a sponged finish in orange and pink water-based paints.

Rag rolling

1 A stippling brush, a stiff, round bristle-headed brush, is useful for many kinds of paint finish, as it helps to distribute the color evenly. Here, a round brush is stiffened by wrapping the head with masking tape.

3 The panel of particle board used in this example has been painted with a pale gray oil-based undercoat and then smoothed with fine sandpaper. The paint and glaze mixture is then painted onto the gray undercoat so that the whole surface is covered.

2 The oil colors are mixed with scumble glaze on a piece of glass (you can also use a palette). An artist's palette knife is used to achieve a thorough mix.

4 The stippling brush is now used to distribute the color in an even film all over the surface. It also provides an interesting background texture.

5 A rag dampened with mineral spirits is then slowly rolled in various directions. This process must be done while the scumble and paint are still wet and can be manipulated easily. When dry, the rolled finish can be smoothed and varnished or waxed.

6 The kind of rag chosen will affect the texture; for example, a rough one such as a face cloth will leave more varied tracks and patterns. You can also experiment with different colors, perhaps using a contrasting undercoat and top coat.

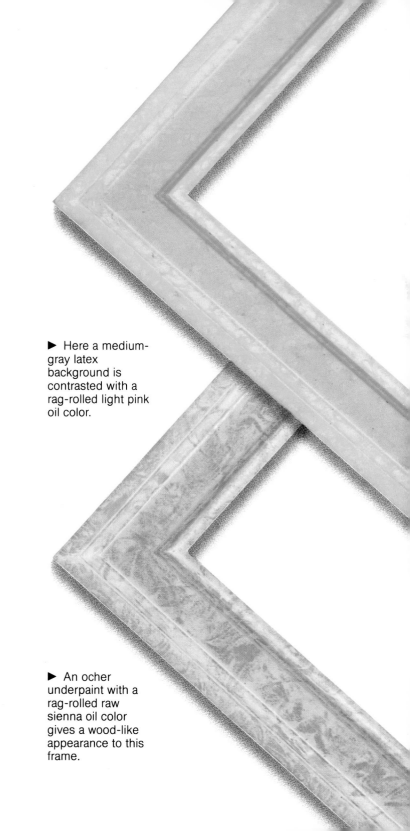

▶ Here a medium-gray latex background is contrasted with a rag-rolled light pink oil color.

▶ An ocher underpaint with a rag-rolled raw sienna oil color gives a wood-like appearance to this frame.

DECOUPAGE

Decoupage, which means decorating a surface with cut pieces of colored paper, is a method which dates back to the 18th century, or possibly even earlier, when paper began to be manufactured in large quantities. Boxes, ornaments, trays, folders, frames, and even walls have been treated in this way, and the effects you can obtain are widely varied.

Any kind of paper can be used, but if you require a smooth, even surface, it should not be too thick or heavily textured. The recent developments in photocopying techniques have greatly increased the possibilities of decoupage. Now it is possible to enlarge an image, print it in color, and adjust the tone to suit the subject.

Pattern books of period designs, now appearing in large numbers, are an excellent source for decoupage; they can be photocopied or used directly from the books. You can also use magazine pages, wallpapers, or marbled papers, either made yourself or obtained from specialist suppliers.

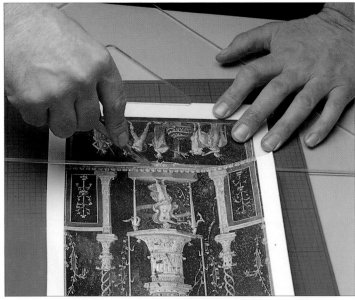

1 A color photograph of a Roman wallpainting formed a suitable decorative motif for the frame. The molding has been measured, and strips are cut to fit.

2 The corners are mitered with a craft knife for a neat appearance. Care must be taken with corners, as an overlap of paper will cause unsightly bumps, particularly if the paper is quite thick.

3 Before gluing, the decoupage paper is held against the molding to check the fit. If any trimming needs to be done, it is easier to do it before the paper is glued down.

4 The back of the paper strip is coated with white paper-glue. Wallpaper paste can also be used, but it takes longer to dry and can cause bubbling.

5 The first paper strip is carefully laid along the molding. The glue does not dry immediately, so small adjustments can be made as you work.

6 The second strip is now put into place, with care taken to make sure that the corners meet properly. When all the paper has been applied, the frame should be given several coats of varnish, either flat or gloss, depending on the effect you want.

▶ In this frame by Isabella Kocum, black and white photocopies taken from some 18th-century engravings were glued on with diluted white glue, and the frame was then varnished.

▼ This mirror frame, made by Jacqueline Beard, is decorated with cutout jelly-jar labels. The background was cracked using "crackleur" varnishes, and brown oil paint was rubbed into the cracks (see Crackle finishes page 92). The frame was then given several layers of varnish to protect the finish and blend the decoupage decorations into the overall surface.

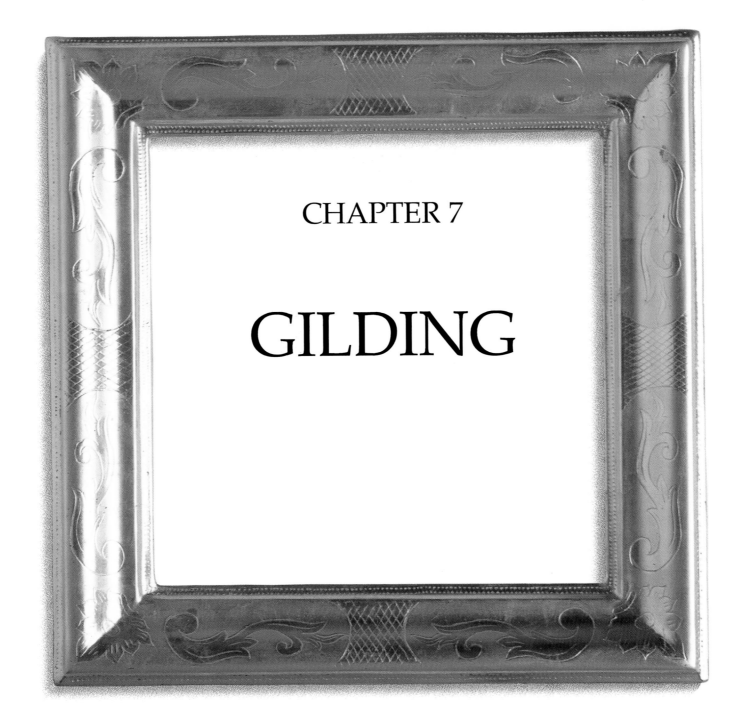

CHAPTER 7

GILDING

Gilding is traditionally done with gold leaf, but gold colors are also made from a mixture of other metals, mainly brass and copper. These imitation golds are obtainable either as fine powders, thin metal leaf, or manufactured into gold paint and gold wax. They are more often used than genuine gold leaf because they are much cheaper and easier to apply, and if the surface of the frame is well prepared, there is no reason why these base-metal "golds" should not make attractive finishes.

However, all forms of gold color will sooner or later tarnish and become much duller. This may take five to ten years, but the gold color will progressively darken through oxidation. Pure gold, on the other hand, whether solid gold or gold leaf, will not tarnish, and has thus been treasured through the ages. A gilded frame may become dusty and dirty with age, but careful cleaning of the gold can restore its brightness (unless the gold has been varnished or lacquered, in which case it is not so easy).

The purity of gold is expressed in "carat," with pure gold being described as 24 carat. Most gilders use 22 carat or $23\frac{1}{2}$ carat, although there are plenty of grades of alloy leaf at 18, 12, and 9 carat. Gold is often mixed with other metals to change the color and to extend the content. For example, white gold is made with silver to produce a warm silver color, while copper is added to gold to make the color more red. There is also lemon gold and green gold.

The purer the gold leaf is, the softer and more malleable it is to use. But, of course, it is also more expensive. Silver, being a heavier and less expensive leaf, is recommended for practice by beginners.

Apart from the purity and color, gold is also differentiated into weight. Suppliers talk of single or double gold. This is slightly confusing, because the double is not usually double the thickness, just heavier. This heavier gold has more covering potential than the single thickness, and when burnished does not show the undercolor of clay.

PREPARING THE SURFACE

Whether you are using real gold leaf or one of the many imitations, it is necessary to have a smooth, even surface to work on. All metal finishes are reflective and will show up any flaws in the surface of the frame very clearly. The most painstaking care is required for the water gilding* method, because the gold is burnished afterward to increase its luster, and this polishing with a burnishing tool requires a smooth and slightly soft surface. The other gold finishes do not need such a demanding surface and can be painted with undercoat or acrylic gesso and then sanded with fine sandpaper.

On all but the most seasoned woods, the corners of the frame are susceptible to movement, which means that in time cracks will appear along the miter. To prevent this, thin strips of fine material should be glued over the joints before the frame is coated with gesso. This is used to fill the grain of the wood and to give a smooth surface for the gold.

Applying gesso
To seal the wood and make it less absorbent, first put on two coats of sizing, allowing drying time between coats. Using a brush, apply eight to ten coats of gesso, always working in the same direction. Allow it to dry slightly but not completely between coats; gesso is stronger if each coat is applied when the last is still slightly damp, so that they combine to form one strong skin.

If air bubbles appear, use a damp finger to rub the gesso lightly between coats.

When the gesso has dried thoroughly, use wet-and-dry sandpaper to sand it smooth. The initial sanding can be done with coarse (180 grit) wet-and-dry sandpaper used with plenty of water. Sand up and down along one side of the frame, and when you can feel the surface is even, wipe off the excess water with cotton. Repeat this procedure on the remaining sides of the frame. The surface is now ready to be sanded with finer sandpaper, starting with 400 grit and finishing with 500 or 600.

✳FURTHER INFORMATION

Water gilding   page 114

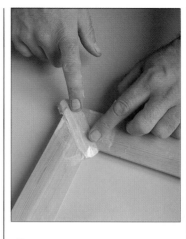

Gesso
1 All wood moves with changes of atmosphere, and gesso is brittle when it is dry, so there is a danger of its cracking along the miter joint. Here the joint has been protected by gluing a strip of silk over it.

2 For a smooth surface, gesso should be put on with a soft brush such as an artist's sable. There are various ways of creating textures if desired (see opposite page), but the gesso must be made thicker.

3 When the gesso is dry, it must be rubbed down with wet-and-dry sandpaper, used with water. It is possible to use dry sandpaper, but it will make a great deal of dust. Rub one side of the frame, continuing until you can feel that the gesso is smooth, then wipe off the excess water with absorbent cotton and repeat the procedure for the other sides.

Engraving

1 Before applying burnishing clay and gold leaf, the gesso can be textured or engraved with a pattern, which makes an interesting contrast to plain areas of burnished leaf. Here a pattern is traced onto a smooth gesso base. Carbon paper can also be used beneath the tracing paper.

2 To make the engraved lines, wet the drawing slightly to soften the gesso, and then score into it with a sharp point. You can use a special engraving tool or improvise one by pushing a nail into a cork. For deep-relief engraving, eight or more coats of gesso need to be applied.

RECIPE FOR GESSO

Ingredients
● Whiting (calcium carbonate, commonly known as chalk). The best is "gilder's whiting," which has been sifted into a fine powder. If coarser whiting is used, it must be sifted and ground in a pestle and mortar.
● Rabbit-skin sizing (glue). This is sold in sheet, granule or fine dust form. The sheets have to be soaked in water overnight, but granules and dust can be mixed to make sizing immediately.

Place in a pan containing warm water, and heat it gently until the granules or powder have dissolved. It is important not to overheat, as this will destroy the adhesion of the sizing.

To make the size
Make a mixture of eight parts water and one part glue. Put into a container (such as an empty coffee can or jar).

To make the gesso
Take the required quantity of warmed sizing and sprinkle in whiting until it settles just below the surface. Stir the mixture slowly and carefully with a brush, taking care not to stir in air bubbles.

TEXTURES UNDER GOLD

Texture underneath gold or silver will form bright highlights that break up the surface and increase the reflected light. In this sample, grains of couscous, sandpaper, and a piece of crochet work have been glued onto a panel, painted with gesso and burnishing clay, and gilded. Between the sandpaper and the crochet material, there is a strip of stippled gesso which has been left as a rough surface.

BURNISHING CLAY

Burnishing clay, or "bole," as it is sometimes called, is used as a preparatory stage to the traditional method of water gilding*. It is applied over the gessoed and sanded surface, and forms a soft bed for the gold leaf. The action of water on the clay also allows the gold leaf to adhere.

It is not necessary to use burnishing clay as an undercoat for transfer gilding* or imitation gold finishes*, but it is widely used for these methods, partly because of its attractive colors and partly because the smooth, satin surface of the clay provides a good foundation for these finishes.

The clay is bought either in liquid form or as a solid cone. The liquid is easier both to obtain and to use; the cones have to be finely ground in a pestle and mortar. The traditional color used under gold leaf is terracotta or red, and either black or blue for silver. Ocher or yellow is often used over ornamental surfaces, so that tiny faults in the gold surface do not show. A choice of other colors is available from specialist suppliers.

Preparation and application
For the first coat, re-heat the sizing solution used in the preparation of gesso* and then dilute it with one part of water to two parts of size solution. Dissolve enough clay into it to give a good color. Apply one coat, and leave to dry completely.

For the following coats, dilute the sizing made for gesso with two parts of water to three parts sizing, and dissolve the clay into it to give the consistency of cream. Apply four coats, allowing each to dry thoroughly and keeping the clay warm throughout. When the last coat has dried, sand carefully with wet-and-dry sandpaper or fine (0000) steel wool to obtain a smooth, silky, and evenly colored surface.

*FURTHER INFORMATION

Water gilding	page 114
Transfer gilding	page 118
Imitation gold finishes	page 127

Gilding and painting
1 The whole frame has been gessoed and rubbed to a smooth finish. In this example, the central margin of the frame will be used for a decorative paint finish with two gold strips on each side, so the burnishing clay is applied only to those areas.

2 Four coats of clay are necessary as a foundation for gilding. Full drying time must be allowed between each coat, and the clay must be kept warm throughout. When the last coat has dried, rub down the clay with 0000 steel wool. If there are any lumps or texture, they may have to be removed with fine sandpaper.

3 The central margin is painted with a crimson acrylic as an undercoat for the decorative paint finish. Gilding can be done before or after the paint finish. Both methods are used, and both have advantages and disadvantages.

2 A first coat of burnishing clay is applied with a sable brush. This will dry more quickly than subsequent coats (in about ten to twenty minutes) as it is absorbed into the gesso. The clay changes color as it dries, so you will know when to paint the next coat.

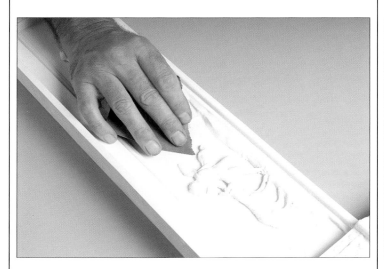

Preparing for gilding
1 The gesso on top of the composition figures has been rubbed smooth in preparation for the burnishing clay. This is a difficult task over an ornamented surface, so careful painting of the gesso is essential to avoid a tedious rubbing-down process.

3 The subsequent coats are made creamier with more clay and slightly less glue. Keep the clay warm as you paint each layer, and do not overload your brush. The final coat is left to dry and then rubbed to a smooth silky finish, using 0000 steel wool and 600 grade sandpaper.

WATER GILDING

Water gilding is the traditional method of gilding, in which the gold or silver leaf is laid onto a surface prepared with gesso and burnishing clay and then burnished with a special tool to give a brilliant luster. The only adhesive used is "gilder's water," which is simply water with a minute amount of glue added. The action of the water on the clay causes the very thin leaves to stick, and the lack of glue allows an even-pressured polish with the burnisher.

The process requires both patience and skill, but is the most highly prized of the gilt finishes. In addition to the gold or silver leaves, you will need a gilder's pad, knife, and tip, as shown in the photograph.

Mixing the gilder's water correctly is crucial; too much glue can result in unattractive brown marks on the leaf. Put a pea-sized piece of the glue mixed for gesso* into half a pint of water, heat gently until dissolved, and when cool add three tablespoons of ethyl or dematured alcohol.

Deposit some leaves of gold at the back of the pad, holding the book open with both hands so that the gold falls easily, then lift a leaf with the knife, place it at the front and breathe gently on it to flatten it before cutting to the required dimension with a firm, even pressure.

Vigorously brush your hair or cheek with the gilder's tip, which should deposit enough oil on it to allow you to pick up the gold, then pick it up with about ³⁄₈ inch showing at the top of the tip, and leave it there while you brush over the clay with plenty of gilder's water. If you find the leaf does not adhere to the tip, rub a little vaseline on your wrist and lightly brush the tip over it, but use it very sparingly, as too much vaseline will prevent the leaf from being released cleanly onto the frame.

Place the gold carefully into position. It will be released from the brush as soon as it makes contact with the clay. Repeat the procedure again, allowing the leaves to overlap slightly, and after you have finished a "run" along one side, gently press the leaves with a ball of cotton.

Leave the leaf for at least two hours before burnishing. To do this, press the agate lightly over the leaf, slightly increasing the pressure and testing the surface as you work. To achieve a uniform luster, it is best to burnish the whole frame lightly and then go over it again with greater pressure.

✻FURTHER INFORMATION

Recipe for gesso   page 111

Gilding equipment
It is possible to improvise a gilding kit using some suede or fine leather glued to a board, and a kitchen knife with an even, but not too sharp, edge. However, for anyone contemplating a large amount of gilding, it is better and more convenient to buy a professional set of tools like the ones shown here. A gilder's cushion with a draft barrier attached means that loose gold can be kept at the back. A gilder's knife has an even but slightly dull blade. It cuts the gold cleanly without damaging the cushion. A gilder's tip is used to pick up the gold leaf. These come in a variety of sizes and qualities. A gilder's mop brush is used to press the gold into awkward areas. A burnishing stick is made of agate set in a wooden handle. A book of loose-leaf gold usually has 25 leaves approximately 3¹⁄₈ in (8cm) square.

Gilding a panel
1 Gilder's water is brushed onto the surface of the clay to help the gold leaf adhere to it. Be generous with the gilder's water.

2 It is best to pick up the gold from the pad with the gilder's tip before applying the water. The gold will stick to the tip until it is released onto the frame. If you paint the water on first and then pick up the gold, there is a danger that the water will have dried too much.

4 To pick up the gold, brush the gilder's tip across your hair or face, which picks up just enough oil for the gold to stick. Then place the tip firmly on the leaf, leaving a small border visible, and lift the brush from the pad.

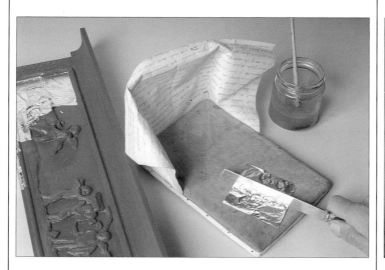

3 Until you are practiced at gilding and can pick up whole squares of gold with confidence, it is easier to cut up the leaves of gold into small pieces. They are less tricky to lift and put into place. Here the gilder's knife is pushed firmly back and forth, cutting the gold cleanly.

5 The leaf will be released from the brush as soon as it touches the dampened clay. After a few minutes, it can be pressed flat, using a piece of cotton, and additional pieces laid, allowing each to overlap slightly.

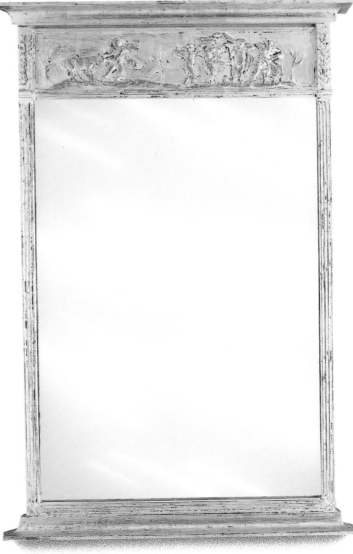

6 The agate tools used for burnishing are made in various shapes and sizes to suit different molding profiles. The broad, flat area is used – do not dig in with the tip. Rub gently at first to test the softness of the gesso, and then gradually build up the pressure until a bright, overall luster is achieved.

▲ This cassetta-style frame made by Patrick Ireland has a water-gilded sight edge and an ivory gesso border divided into plates. The inner glazed frame and border are surrounded by a black-lacquered "Hogarth" frame with gilt ball decoration.

7 For this frame, the final stage was to distress the gold leaf with beeswax, particularly the figures at the top. The background of the top panel was coated with acrylic varnish to give a contrasting flat finish.

The frame is tabernacle style, with the top panel decorated with Neo-classical putti and fluted pillars on the sides. The top and bottom are faced with coving.

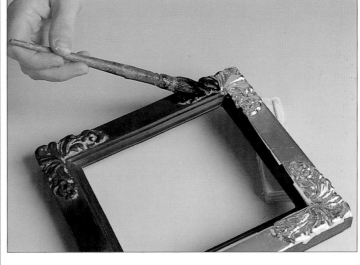

Gilding ornament

1 Applying leaf over decoration is trickier than laying it on a flat surface, as there can be a problem with covering all the recesses. If these are painted with a light yellow ocher clay a similar tone and color to the gold, it will be less noticeable if the gold does not quite reach the bottom of the recess.

3 In awkward areas of the corner decoration, a gilder's mop is used to press the gold into place. This is an invaluable tool, which can also be used to clean off excess pieces of gold.

2 In this example the relief decoration on the corners is quite deep. Black burnishing clay was painted all over the frame before the corner recesses were coated in yellow. The leaf is then laid in the same way as in the previous demonstration.

4 The gold continues to be laid all around the frame, starting with the top edge. After burnishing, it will be distressed to reveal some of the black clay color underneath. The areas normally chosen for distressing are the highest parts, such as the "peaks" of the decoration, thus artificially simulating a process which would occur naturally with time.

TRANSFER GILDING

The main difference between transfer gilding and water gilding is that glue is used in the latter process instead of gilder's water, which makes it impossible to burnish the leaf. The luster is thus less bright, but transfer gilding has many advantages. It is considerably faster (and is thus the process used for most commercially made predecorated moldings); it is more robust; and because it is not burnished, the gesso surface does not need such elaborate preparation.

The leaf sold for transfer gilding is backed with paper, hence the name of the process, but you can also use loose leaf. The traditional glue is a viscous substance called oil gold size, but in recent times a water-soluble glue has been developed, which is easier to use and more flexible in terms of drying time (gold size dries quickly).

However, gold size is stronger, so is better for any gilding that may be subject to stress. It must be painted evenly onto the surface to be gilded, as otherwise the thinner areas of glue will be ready for gilding before the rest. It should be just a little tacky, so test it by placing your knuckle or the back of your hand against it. If it pulls too obviously, wait a little longer before laying the leaf.

Water-based glue will be ready for the leaf fifteen minutes after application, and since it stays usable for much longer, you do not need to rush with the gilding.

Both types of glue are suitable for transfer leaf, loose leaf, and the heavier imitation metal leafs*.

FURTHER INFORMATION

Imitation gold
finishes   page 127

Using gold leaf

1 It is not necessary to use gesso on a frame that is to be transfer gilded, but it should be painted with some form of undercoat. Here a thick undercoat of black casein paint was used (black burnishing clay is frequently used underneath water-gilded silver). A water-based gold size, a modern alternative to the oil gold size used in the past, was painted evenly on top of the black paint.

2 After about fifteen minutes, the water size is dry enough to start laying the leaf. Transfer leaf is the same as loose leaf, except it has been pressed onto transparent paper, which makes it easier to apply.

Using imitation gold

1 This frame is a traditional Hogarth type, which usually has a black central margin and a gilded outer edge and sight edge. The sight edge has been painted with terracotta clay to resemble the traditional gilded finish. Water gold size is now applied on top preparatory to gilding.

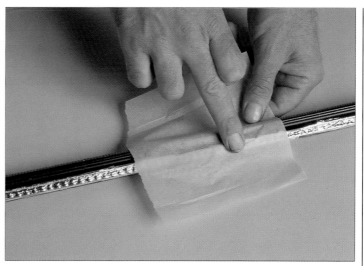

2 The imitation gold leaf (sometimes called "Dutch" or "schlagg" leaf) used in this example is loose rather than paper-backed leaf. It can be cut into the appropriate sizes with a craft knife.

4 To press the leaf firmly over the underlying ornament, tissue or thin plastic can be used as a barrier so that no glue is transferred to the fingers. This makes it easier to stick the gold closely to the surface of the frame. Imitation gold and silver leaf, and silver alloy leaves need to be protected from tarnishing by applying coats of shellac or other specialist lacquers.

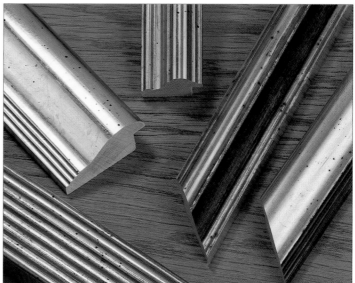

3 Unlike genuine gold or silver leaf, this can be picked up with the fingers and placed into position, or thin cardboard can be folded and used as tweezers to pick it up.

Commercial moldings
A wide variety of ready-made gilded moldings are available from framing suppliers.

PASTIGLIA

This is a thick gesso* suitable for ornamental work on frames. The ratio of glue to water is the same as the recipe given on the previous pages, the difference being that more whiting is used. For ordinary gesso, the glue was filled almost to the surface with whiting, but in this case whiting is added until a thick, creamy mixture is obtained.

There are many fine examples of pastiglia work on period Italian frames. This technique can also be used for creating a more contemporary ornamental surface. Pastiglia is usually applied on top of a previously gessoed and sanded surface, and then gilded.

The characteristic appearance of pastiglia is one in which the ornament appears almost to have grown out of the gesso. It is an ideal technique for achieving fine pattern work.

❋FURTHER INFORMATION

Recipe for gesso   page 111

1 A pattern was chosen from a book of designs and then traced. A simple, bold pattern is most suitable for pastiglia decoration; too many intricate details are difficult to execute, at least until you are practiced.

2 The traced design is now transferred to the frame. It is usual to apply pastiglia decoration to a surface already prepared with gesso, as this makes it easier to smooth the pattern. This frame has had eight coats of gesso, rubbed smooth.

3 The thick pastiglia mixture is painted onto the drawn design. Do not apply too much at once; but build up the three-dimensional shapes gradually. The pastiglia gesso is so thick, however, that three or four coats will produce a substantial depth. It should not be allowed to dry in between coats; you can apply another one as soon as the glossy wet shine has disappeared.

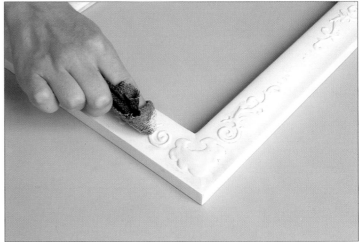

4 When the design is complete, but before the pastiglia is fully dry, rub it with a damp and slightly textured cloth. This smooths it out and is much easier than rubbing down an ornamented surface when it is hard and dry.

5 When the pastiglia is quite dry, it may be necessary to do some final finishing with dry sandpaper before applying the burnishing clay. Four coats of terracotta burnishing clay are painted onto the surface; each is allowed to dry before the next is applied.

6 Gilder's water is brushed onto the clay, and the gold or silver leaf is laid on the wet clay. The transfer gilding method can also be used, but the bright burnished surface achieved by water gilding and burnishing shows pastiglia ornament to the best advantage.

7 The gold has been cut into appropriate sized pieces, which are picked up and lifted onto the frame with a gilder's tip.

8 The brilliant luster achieved by burnishing displays the pastiglia ornament to advantage. It can sometimes overwhelm a picture, however, and various methods can be used after burnishing for dulling or distressing it.

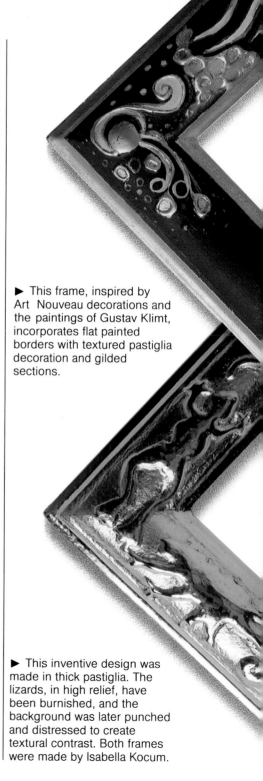

▶ This frame, inspired by Art Nouveau decorations and the paintings of Gustav Klimt, incorporates flat painted borders with textured pastiglia decoration and gilded sections.

▶ This inventive design was made in thick pastiglia. The lizards, in high relief, have been burnished, and the background was later punched and distressed to create textural contrast. Both frames were made by Isabella Kocum.

FINISHES OVER GILDING

Burnished gold leaf is very bright and lustrous, an effect which is not suitable for all pictures – it can be overpowering. Gilders have devised a variety of different techniques for reducing the brilliance of the gold and subtly toning the surface.

Distressing gold and silver

This involves rubbing off some of the leaf to expose the clay beneath, which gives a pleasing mature color to the gold or silver. It is much easier to distress water-gilded* leaf than transfer leaf* because there is very little glue used in the water-gilding process. The amount you distress the leaf is a matter of personal taste. On some frames, it is so distressed that only the double-thickness overlap across both leaves is left. More often, however, the leaf is lightly rubbed to hint at the color below.

Flat and color effects

The simplest method of producing a flat finish while preserving the color of the leaf is to leave certain areas unburnished. You can see this effect on the frame illustrated on page 108, where only the ornamental motifs have been burnished. The unburnished areas are more vulnerable to damage, and so a thin coat of shellac* is often used on top. You can also dull the surface of burnished gold by painting shellac, flat acrylic varnish, or a thin solution of rabbit-skin sizing* over it.

Tortoiseshell effect

The traditional method was to lay real tortoiseshell over a silver ground, which was often tinted red to give a richer color below the shell. The same applies to the fake plastic tortoiseshell used here; a silver ground gives a more brilliant translucence. Another type of tortoiseshell effect is made with earth colors suspended in shellac and dropped onto a silver surface.

Sgraffito

This is another traditional technique, in which egg tempera color is laid over a gilded finish and then scratched to reveal the gold beneath. Tempera is ideal because it does not adhere strongly to the gold, but other water-based colors such as acrylic and casein can also be used for this technique.

*FURTHER INFORMATION

Water gilding	page 114
Transfer gilding	page 118
Rabbit-skin sizing, see	
Recipe for gesso	page 111
Paints, mediums,	
and varnishes	page 86

▲ Distressed gold
The effects you can obtain by distressing gold and silver leaf are extremely varied. Here the gold has been distressed to a flat finish which marries well with the bands of paintwork in the recesses of the molding. The small specks of burnishing clay showing through the gold give an attractive slightly textured effect.

Painted tortoiseshell

1 A group of earth pigments have been mixed with shellac and painted onto a silvered frame. For this process it is best to limit the color range, and here only three are used, yellow ocher, burnt sienna, and raw umber. As with the other painted imitation finishes, it is useful to have some reference material on hand, either photographs or the real thing. Unless attention is paid to the distinctive markings, this finish can bear more resemblance to leopard skin.

2 The colors need to be kept wet by spraying with denatured alcohol so that they can be manipulated with thin plastic bags, feathers, or rags, as in the marble and lapis lazuli finishes shown in the previous chapter. When the textured background pattern is formed, you can start to paint in the distinctive dark markings, which are usually rounded at the edges and merge into one another.

3 When enough marks have been made, the shellac must be allowed to dry thoroughly; this will take twenty-four hours. The finish is then rubbed smooth using fine grades of wet-and-dry sandpaper and steel wool. Some top coats of shellac can be applied to give a smooth finish, and can be tinted with color to harmonize with the overall effect. For a silk finish, rub some steel wool with wax over the frame and polish with a dusting cloth.

This oval frame, made by Robert Cunning, has an undercolor of imitation metal leaf, which reflects light through the paint finish. The tortoiseshell markings were made with oil color and scumble glaze, and warm earth colors were stippled and feathered onto the gold ground. When the paint was dry, the frame was rubbed smooth and then waxed.

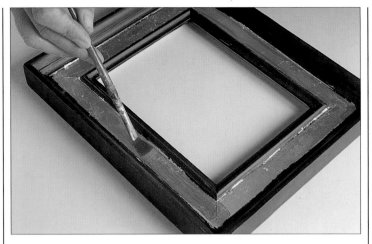

Artificial tortoiseshell

1 The frame was first painted with a black undercoat and then transfer gilded with silver leaf. A red shellac varnish is painted onto the silver prior to sticking down the plastic tortoiseshell. The silver ground will reflect light through the tortoiseshell, which would otherwise be dull and lackluster. The red shellac seals the silver and prevents tarnishing, but also has a decorative function, giving a richer light to the tortoiseshell. The method shown here is the traditional one used in the past for real tortoiseshell on frames.

3 Thin strips have been cut to fit the central margin of the frame, and the corners are now trimmed to a 45° angle to form a miter joint. Tortoiseshell frames were popular in 17th-century Holland. The shell often came in short plates that were attached to the flat borders of ebony frames.

4 A strong glue is needed to attach the plastic to the frame, and contact adhesive is used here. On period frames the plates were held by small pieces of ebony beading.

2 Tortoiseshell is now a prohibited import, so plastic imitations must be used instead. It resembles the genuine article in texture, depth, and color, and can be very effective. It is easy to cut with a sharp craft knife.

5 The contact adhesive is applied to both surfaces, left for a few minutes to allow the glue to harden a little, and the two surfaces brought together. The plastic tortoiseshell has the advantage of needing no other protection or finish, and its semi-matte surface closely resembles real tortoiseshell.

Sgraffito

1 The frame was water gilded and burnished before covering with four coats of ultramarine egg tempera and left to dry. The design was transferred to the paint by tracing with a soft pencil, and the engraving was made by working over the traced design with a sharpened piece of wood.

▲ In this frame made by Isabella Kocum, silver leaf was burnished and then distressed to reveal red burnishing clay. Blue acrylic paint was then laid on top and scratched away to make the silver and red pattern.

▶ A classical running wave pattern has been scratched through black tempera paint to reveal the water-gilded surface underneath. The frame was made by Isabella Kocum.

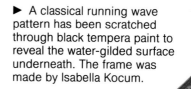

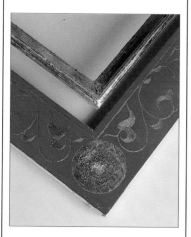

2 When the sgraffito design was complete, circles of decorative stars were punched in the corners (the punching method is shown overleaf).

▶ This copy of an 18th-century Italian frame made by Robert Cunning has sgraffito acanthus-leaf decoration in the corners and center.

PUNCHED AND ENGRAVED DESIGNS

Breaking up the surface of the gold or silver, either by making punch marks after gilding or by engraving into the gesso before gilding, can give more light and variety of texture to the frame.

An ordinary nail set will leave a circular pattern in the gold which when repeated as an overall design can be very attractive. More elaborate punch motifs can be purchased from specialist shops.

Gesso is a soft surface and can be very easily textured by making scratched designs; the thicker it is, the deeper your scratch marks can be. Other methods include stippling with a thick gesso mix and sticking textured fabric onto the wood before applying the gesso.

The engraved pattern on this frame by Isabella Kocum was made in the gesso before gilding. The delicate design is reinforced by the contrast of textures; only the areas inside the engraved lines have been burnished.

▼ Punched designs
Punching is usually done after gilding. This frame has been gilded in silver leaf over a pastiglia design, and a close pattern of punch marks provides a contrast to the burnished highlights. The leaf is not broken by the punch, but pressed into the soft gesso beneath, so you can hit it quite hard.

✳FURTHER INFORMATION

Recipe for gesso   page 111

IMITATION GOLD FINISHES

Those who do not want to spend a great deal of time and money on a perfect gold finish may find one of the various imitation golds a useful alternative. Manufacturers now produce very convincing imitation gold and silver leafs, which can be almost indis-tinguishable from the real thing. Unfortunately, they do tarnish and need to be protected with a varnish or lacquer, which robs the finish of the subtlety and glow of real gold or silver. They are applied using glue, as described in the section on transfer gilding.

Gold paint can be obtained ready made, or you can mix your own using bronze powders and a medium such as shellac, white glue, or rabbit-skin glue. These powders are usually made from bronze and are thus called bronze powders, but they have the appearance of gold or silver and are made in a variety of colors and qualities. The best, called burnishing powders, are finely ground, and when suspended in shellac make a quick-drying and effective paint.

Gold and silver waxes can produce an effect very similar to real metal leaf if applied over a surface prepared with gesso and burnishing clay.

Applying the gold
1 For the best results, gold wax should be applied with a soft rag over a surface prepared with gesso and burnishing clay.

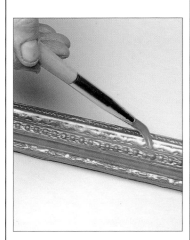

2 It can then be burnished with an agate tool in the usual way. The gold used here is that made to the recipe shown on the right. It is thicker and more lustrous than most ready-made gold waxes.

RECIPE FOR GOLD OR SILVER WAX

Materials
- Carnauba wax
- Beeswax
- Turpentine or mineral spirits
- Bronze powder

Method
Place beeswax and carnauba wax (in a proportion of approximately four of beeswax to one of carnauba) in a coffee can.

Cover with turpentine or mineral spirits and heat gently in a saucepan of water.

When the waxes have melted, test the mixture by pouring a little onto a non-absorbent surface such as glass or plastic. It should solidify in about ten seconds. If it sets almost immediately, it is too hard, so add more mineral spirits. If it takes too long to set, add more wax.

When the mixture is right, use a knife to mix in as much powder as you can until it becomes crumbly. Store in an airtight jar or can. The wax is usually applied with a rag or a finger, but can be thinned with mineral spirits to make a paint.

CHAPTER 8

RESTORATION AND REPAIR

Old frames are often poorly preserved, with their gilding, paint, or other decorative finishes cracked, chipped, and weathered. Most old wood frames can be cleaned and restored quite easily, though frames with decoration on a gesso surface may present more of a problem, particularly if they have been kept in a damp place. Moisture tends to crack and soften gesso, and this can make restoration impossible.

A lot of the frames bought from auctions and antique shops are of the 19th and early 20th centuries. They are usually made of ornamental composition in gold or silver, or plain wood with a paint or gilt finish over a gesso ground. Even the most humble frames in the 19th century were gilded, often in silver with a yellow wash to emulate gold.

Although such frames may not be particularly valuable, they are worth preserving and restoring as long as they are not too badly damaged. Some frames, unfortunately, are so far gone in decay that it is not worth the time and expense. If the gesso is flaking off in large lumps, this usually means that the adhesion between the wood and the gesso has deteriorated to the point that it is no longer worth renovating. In this case, the frame itself may still be usable, and if it is an attractive shape, it is worth soaking off the gesso and composition. This is easily done by wrapping wet rags around the frame and leaving overnight to soften. In the morning the gesso and composition will scrape off easily.

For valuable carved and molded frames, it is best to seek expert advice before attempting restoration, as a poor repair can reduce the value of the frame. A useful standard to apply is that any restoration should be invisible, and if possible repaired with the same materials as the original frame.

CLEANING FRAMES

Old frames usually need to be cleaned, but unless great care is taken, there is a risk of destroying the patina of age, which can be an attractive feature, or of removing areas of gilding. For wood and painted frames, a light cleaning mixture of ammonia and water (one part ammonia to eight parts water) is all that is generally required. When dry, the frame can be polished with wax. If you want to remove varnish from the surface, you will have to use the appropriate solvent. There are several brands of general-purpose paint and varnish removers, which can be thinned with water or oil depending on the type. This will give you more control during the cleaning process.

When cleaning an old gilt frame, even more care is needed. The leaf is so thin that a heavy hand or a strong solution of cleaner can remove the gilt completely in a matter of seconds. It is safer to start with a weak solution of cleaner, which unless there is a top layer of lacquer or varnish, is usually ammonia and water. Try a mix of sixteen parts water to one of ammonia, and if this is not effective, add more ammonia. Apply the cleaner lightly with a brush and then gently dab off the moisture with cotton. Be careful not to wipe with the cotton, as this too can lift the gold leaf.

For gold or silver which has been lacquered or varnished, try using acetone or denatured alcohol in a similarly careful way. If this does not work, then try one of the commercial brands of paint and varnish remover, suitably diluted.

Antique patina

When you have cleaned the surface and repaired* any damage, there remains the problem of matching the antique patina. Sometimes a little color pigment added to wax and then rubbed onto the cleaned part is sufficient, but for larger areas it may be easier to use color in the form of paint.

2 While the frame is still wet, lightly dab with cotton balls to lift the dirt. Do not rub with the cotton; this may remove the gold as well.

1 Apply the diluted ammonia with a paintbrush, working over a small area at a time, and pushing the brush into the crevices of the molding. If the ammonia mixture starts to remove any of the gilded surface, dilute it with more water, but if the dirt is stubborn, add more ammonia.

3 When the frame is clean, it is important to neutralize any residue of ammonia with water. Work over the frame with clean water and a brush, and then dab again with cotton balls.

This could either be a solution of rabbit-skin glue* mixed with watercolor or dry pigment, or oil paint used very thinly in the form of a glaze. The advantage of glue and watercolor is that it can be removed or modified without damaging the surface; just apply warm water carefully on a brush.

A quick way to mellow the surface of gold or silver is to apply walnut-colored Danish oil. This can be rubbed on with a cloth or painted with a brush; to reduce the effect, wipe it down with a cloth dipped in mineral spirits. A thin film of this black-brown color is effective as an aging patina and lends a subtle darkness to the gilding. On silver, you can obtain a similar effect by applying a chemical, ammonium hydrosulfide. It should be used sparingly or the silver will turn very dark, or you can thin it with water before application, to reduce this effect. The smell of sulfur is not pleasant, so keep the lid on as much as possible.

To distress either paint or transfer gilding*, use fine steel wool and a cutting compound such as pumice or rottenstone. This polishes the surface and can remove a little of the top coat to reveal the color below.

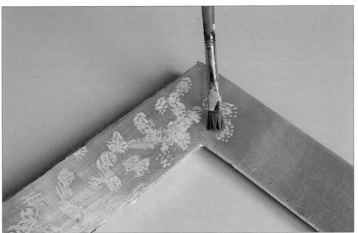

Ammonium hydrosulfide

1 New silver looks very bright, but will tarnish to a dull brown or black if it is left unprotected. Some discoloration will occur after a few months, and this can look attractive. The frame can then be protected with lacquer to prevent further tarnishing. Here the discoloring process is artificially induced by using hydrosulfide to patinate a newly made silver-gilt frame.

2 The undiluted chemical will turn the silver dark brown, so for lighter effects it needs to be diluted with water. It takes an hour or more for the chemical to react fully, after which it must be neutralized with water, or it will continue to darken the silver.

Bitumen

Another way to darken silver or gold is to apply bitumen paint. This heavy brown color is painted on the gilt surface with a brush and then lightly wiped off with a cloth. It dries quickly, so work in small areas, wiping it off as you progress around the frame. When dry, the bitumen can be easily removed with mineral spirits or turpentine.

REPAIR AND REJOINING

Many old frames are so well constructed that the miter joints remain tight even though the glue has deteriorated. This is usually because there is a brace of some kind across the miter. If there are no obvious gaps in the joints, it is safer to leave them alone, but if there are gaps, and the frame is still nailed together, you can often put glue into the joints without removing the nails. The large tapered nails often used on old frames are difficult to extract without damaging the corners. If the joints are badly damaged, it may be necessary to pull the frame apart, trim the miters, and reassemble.

The most commonly used glue in restoration work is the animal-based carpenter's glue, known as hide glue. This is useful because it can be softened by heat, and if any adjustment needs to be made, a kitchen knife heated over a flame and then inserted into the joint will loosen the bond so that it can be shifted.

Although still used by restorers and other craftsmen, hide glue has largely been replaced by white glue, which requires no heat, dries quickly, and is transparent when dry.

Re-gluing
1 In this frame the old glue had deteriorated, but the nails still held the frame together although the joints were loose. Rather than damage the frame by extracting the nails, fresh white glue was put into the joint.

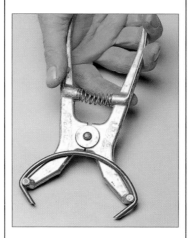

2 Spring miter clamps are useful for clamping the corners securely while the glue dries.

3 Although the clamps do leave small marks on the corners, they are adaptable and can be used to exert pressure on different areas of the frame. This is an advantage with old frames, because often the wood has warped and a lot of pressure is needed to obtain a tight joint.

4 While the clamp is still in place, new nails are hammered into the corner to strengthen the joint. It is safer to drill holes first, as otherwise you may split the wood when hammering. Any marks can be filled and colored to blend into the side of the frame.

Before and after
This early 19th-century frame was extensively damaged, particularly in the corners. Molds (see pages 134-135) were made of the existing pieces of ornament, and then one complete corner was molded and modeled. The other three corners were then made from a mold of this corner. The frame was cleaned with ammonia and water, and all the repairs were re-gilded and then colored to match the existing patina.

REPLACING BROKEN ORNAMENT

Although some minor repairs can be made to a chipped frame by modeling with a knife and filler, any pattern or ornament must be remade and replaced. This is done by making a mold from an undamaged area of the frame, taking an impression and then gluing the new piece onto the frame. Usually, the ornament is in fairly shallow relief and can be reproduced using one-piece molds.

Making the mold
There are many materials from which molds can be made. In the past, carved box-wood molds were used, later superseded by industrial gelatin and plaster. We now have, among other substances, fiberglass, latex rubber, and silicone rubber. Fiberglass, used by professional moldmakers, is messy and gives off noxious fumes, so is not suitable for home use. Molds can also be made from wax, epoxy resin, and modeling clay. They do not give fine definition, but are adequate for simple patterns.

Silicone rubber, on the other hand, gives excellent definition and is easy to use. It comes in two parts, the silicone, which is white, and the catalyst, which is colored. The more catalyst you use, the faster the rubber hardens, but care must be taken not to add too much, or it will become "buttery" before a good impression has been obtained.

To give more firmness to the mold, the back is usually given a coat of plaster, but a good alternative to plaster is the kind of silicone rubber that plumbers use around the edges of baths and basins. This is sold in caulking tubes.

For quick-disposable molds, there is a seaweed-based medium used by dentists and the food industry. This is a

Silicone rubber
1 To protect the surface of the frame, apply a light coat of linseed oil to the place where the molding medium is to go.

2 The red catalyst is mixed into the white silicone rubber. With this particular type, the more catalyst you add, the more quickly the rubber will harden.

3 The buttery silicone rubber is applied to the frame with a knife. Make sure that any small cracks and undercuts in the ornament are filled before the rubber is put in place; otherwise, it will be difficult to lift the mold without damaging the frame.

powder which, when mixed with water, forms a firm jelly. It gives a good definition and sets very fast, but unfortunately it does not last more than twenty-four hours and is thus only suitable for small areas of ornament. As with silicone rubber, a firm plaster back will make it easier to take an impression.

Taking the impression
Once the mold has been made, an impression is taken by filling it with some form of composition such as that given in the recipe overleaf. You can

4 When the rubber has set, lift it gently off the frame. Larger molds will benefit from a backing of plaster or more silicone rubber, so that the mold does not distort when an impression is taken.

Alginate
1 Again, linseed oil is applied to protect the surface of the frame before the alginate molding medium is put in place.

2 The seaweed-based medium is mixed to a smooth paste with approximately its own volume of water. It is then applied with a knife. Alginate dries fast, so you must work quickly.

3 Fresh alginate will not combine with alginate that has already set, so the medium is only suitable for small repairs. However, it has good definition. Like silicone rubber, it is flexible, and will need a rigid backing of plaster.

RECIPE FOR COMPOSITION

This is a traditional recipe, variations of which have been used on picture frames for over 200 years.

Ingredients
- Rabbit-skin glue
- Soft toilet paper
- Whiting
- Linseed oil

Method
The main base is a strong mixture of rabbit-skin glue. Mix it in a can heated in a saucepan of water, as in the recipe for gesso, but in a proportion of three parts water to one of glue. When it has melted, remove it from the hot water and put it to one side.

Now take some toilet paper and put it into the water of the saucepan (you will need about five sheets to ½ pint of water), bring to a boil and leave in boiling water for about a minute.

Take out the resulting pulp and leave to cool, then break it up into small pieces and add to the glue. Heat this mixture until thoroughly combined.

Now put in enough whiting to make the consistency of firm bread dough, stirring with a knife until it comes off the sides of the can in lumps.

Finally, add two or three tablespoons of linseed oil and stir again, keeping the composition warm until you begin to use it.

also use plaster for this, but because it cannot be removed from the mold until it is rigid, it can only be attached to a flat surface. The beauty of the composition is that it is malleable and can be draped over a curved frame while still wet without losing any definition.

To prevent the composition from sticking to the mold, first lubricate the latter with a little linseed oil. Flour your hands with some whiting, pick up some of the composition, briefly kneading it with your hands, press it into the mold, and smooth it into shape with a knife dipped in hot water. Leave it for five to ten minutes, and then carefully lift it out (it will still be soft and flexible). It can now be trimmed to fit the repair and glued into position using rabbit-skin glue* in a proportion of three parts water to one of glue.

It is important to obtain the right thickness of composition for the repair, so mix it carefully. If you make a mistake, it is easier to recast the mold than to trim the excess from the back of the impression. Any trimmings of composition can be put back into the pot and re-used.

*FURTHER INFORMATION

Rabbit-skin sizing, see
Recipe for gesso   page 111

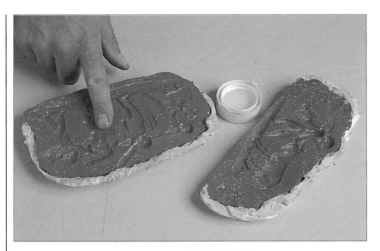

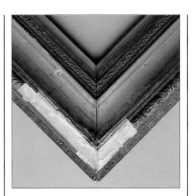

Taking the impression
1 These molds are made of silicone rubber, backed with plaster for extra rigidity. Before putting in the composition, the mold is given a light coating of linseed oil, which helps to release the impression.

2 The composition is put into the mold while it is still warm and flexible. The back is then smoothed with a knife, which is frequently dipped into hot water to prevent sticking. This action also helps to press the composition into the fine detail of the mold.

3 The composition should still be flexible when it is taken out of the mold so that any excess can be easily trimmed, and if required the ornament can be draped over a contoured frame and glued in place. This is a shallow mold so the composition is dry enough to lift after a few minutes. Deeper molds will take longer.

▲ From top to bottom: a frame with a missing cornerpiece which could be cast in composition or plaster. A new composition corner ornament shaped into place. An oval frame with a repair in composition, and an ornament modeled in epoxy resin.

MAKING A REPLICA FRAME

One of the most exciting and challenging projects for the picture framer is the construction and decoration of replicas of authentic period frames. The cost of the genuine articles, particularly from the early Renaissance and pre-Renaissance periods, is so prohibitive that only wealthy collectors can afford them.

If you are framing an old picture, or a reproduction of one, you can discover the type of frame that would have been used by conducting some research into the styles of the period. In recent years more attention has been paid to framing old masters in their appropriate frames, and both major museums and some smaller galleries now buy or reproduce period frames where necessary.

Many of the Old Master pictures in the National Gallery in London, England, are in their original frames or at least in correct period frames, and there are also catalogues from exhibitions of frames – notably the Metropolitan Museum, New York, and the Art Institute of Chicago. These catalogues contain full details of frames, with the scale profiles and accurate dimensions which are necessary for authentic

replicas. Auction houses often have frame sales, for which well-illustrated catalogues are prepared, but the information is less detailed and not always reliable.

Sometimes a replica frame is made for its own sake rather than as a surround for a picture. The frame can be hung on the wall with nothing in it, or used as a mirror frame. Mirrors can be used in almost any style frame, allowing the framer to indulge in the extravagant and the ornamental without restraint. A selection of mirror frames can be seen on pages 156-159.

Attaching ornament
1 This corner mold has been taken from a carved 18th-century panel frame. When the composition is taken from the mold, it is still wet enough to cut easily. Here the excess composition is being trimmed from the elaborate cut-out corner. The waste pieces of composition can be put back into the pot and re-used.

2 The molded ornament is glued onto the frame while it is still flexible. A strong mixture of rabbit-skin glue (three of water to one of glue) should be used for this. It is usually easier to attach ornament to a frame which has first been gessoed and smoothed.

Gilded ornament
These two frame corners show a before and after stage, with the one at the top awaiting gilding. The bottom example has been gilded on the patterned design, and the background has been painted green.

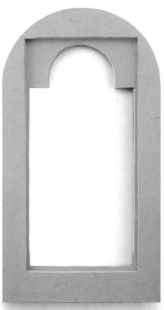

2 Another piece of board was cut for the back of the frame, and the two pieces were glued and screwed together. The back board creates a rabbet for the mirror as well as giving extra strength and depth to the frame.

3 Pastiglia decoration based on 10th-century Iraqi ceramic designs was added to all the sides, and the frame was gilded in white gold over a blue clay ground. The top and bottom backgrounds have been left unburnished and coated with a weak solution of rabbit-skin glue. The frame was made by Aristotelis Zabetas.

Using composite board
1 This replica of a Gothic arched frame has been cut out of medium-density fiber board (MDF). The window and the rounded sight edge were cut and profiled with a router.

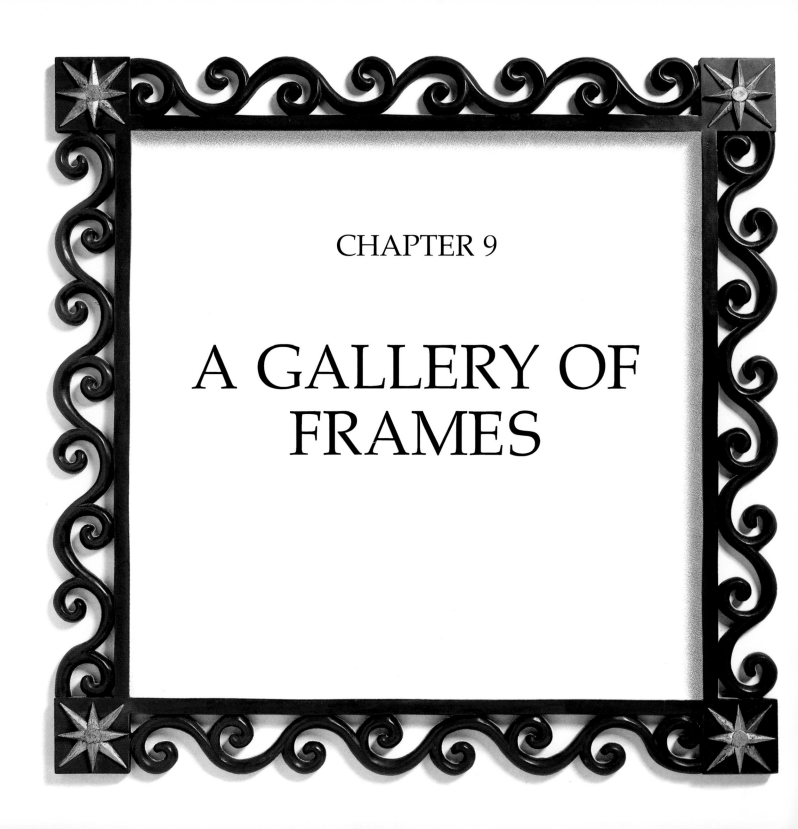

CHAPTER 9

A GALLERY OF FRAMES

This chapter is intended as an inspiration to the framemaker, showing the various possibilities that can be explored.

Although there are traditional styles, many of which are still appropriate, there is no one perfect way to frame any picture. Two main factors have to be considered. The frame must suit the picture and enhance our viewing of it, but it must also serve a protective function, whether the picture is a work on paper, an oil painting, an embroidery, or some other type of image or object. Sometimes, however, the frame can have more importance than the picture. A color reproduction, for instance, or a black and white engraving from a pattern book, could become simply one element in a frame which is conceived as a piece of furniture in its own right. This is particularly true of mirror frames; because there is no image, the frame can be made in any style that the maker pleases.

WORKS ON PAPER

Most watercolors, pastels, prints, drawings, and photographs need glass to protect them, and a mount or slip frame to separate the glass from the picture and prevent the two from sticking together. The frames are usually light in construction to suit the delicacy of the image.

Watercolors

The delicate, transparent quality of watercolor calls for a discreet framing style. Traditional 19th-century watercolors often had wide neutral margins of matboard, sometimes with line and wash* decorations harmonizing with colors in the picture. Thin gilt frames with small floral ornaments were popular, among other styles, and added a restrained richness to the subdued tones of the watercolor.

Modern watercolors are often brighter and more vibrant than their predecessors, and call for a bolder display. Color washes* over the frame can be attractive and can be used to echo colors in the picture. Natural and colored wood, as well as more contemporary finishes such as bright enamel and metallic frames, are widely used, as are colored mats.

◄ The simple shape and warm tones of this natural wood frame work well with the strong 19th-century watercolor by Peter de Wint. A more complex treatment, or a decorated or colored mat, could have lessened its impact.

◄ Ray Willingham has framed his own watercolor with a discreet natural-wood molding, which contrasts nicely with the pale green of the mat. The mat has a white inner border with a gold pen line separating the two colors.

▶ Adèle Seigal's watercolor is strong enough to benefit from an unusual treatment – a distressed gilt frame and no mat. The gold leaf has been distressed most heavily at the sight edge, where the visible underlayer of red burnishing clay echoes the warm red-browns in the painting. The frame was made by Harry Seigal.

◀ A backmounting method has been used here, with the picture mounted on one piece of matboard and the main window mat cut from another. This gives an effect similar to that of a floating frame (see page 49), where the edges of the picture are not hidden by a rabbet or the edges of the mat. The treatment gives additional importance to the small image, further enhanced by the wide reverse-bevel gilt molding. The painting is by Andrew Hewkin and the frame by James Frames (James Sullivan).

There is an ever-increasing choice of colored matboard, in both vivid and subdued colors, which can be used to complement both the frame and the picture.

Pastels

Pastels, being an older medium than watercolor, have a longer tradition of framing. The richness of the chalk colors is closer to oil painting than to watercolor, and can stand a bolder framed display. Traditionally, pastels were framed in similar surrounds to oil paintings, though the moldings were usually thinner. They were glazed and separated from the glass by concealed blocks of wood. No mats were used, although sometimes decorated slip frames performed the same function.

Unlike watercolors, pastels do not fade with time, but they are extremely vulnerable to surface damage and need the protection of a well-made frame. Many pastellists fix their work before framing, but others do not, as fixative has a darkening effect on the colors. Even when fixed, the soft pigment can easily smudge and fall off the paper surface. These days, pastels are usually framed like watercolors, with mats and a similar style of molding. This suits some delicate works, but a more dramatic presentation can be tried for the stronger styles.

Prints

The traditional print frame was even more reserved than the period watercolor frame. Etchings and engravings had ivory or pale gray mats lightly decorated with pen and wash lines. The frame was often thin

▲ This strong and colorful pastel painting called for an equally positive framing treatment. The frame was hand-colored by Adèle Seigal with gouache paints and given a brilliant red sight edge, which both picks up colors in the painting and separates the frame from the dark blue mat.

◄ The warmth of the terracotta and gold in this distressed gilt frame combines well with this engraving, the sepia tones of a Leonardo drawing.

flat wood, gessoed and black-lacquered. This somber style of frame is less favored now, but it suits monochrome prints very well, as does the "Hogarth" style frame, a variation of the same type, but with small gilt beadings on each side of the black molding.

Bolder contemporary prints need a more solid approach. Wider natural-wood frames are frequently used, and so are colored moldings and matboard. Smaller prints can be enhanced by using wide mats, which has the effect of focusing attention on a small image.

Maps and documents
These have traditionally been framed in natural wood. At the turn of this century, there was a fashion for bird's-eye maple veneer and other exotic woods, with gold or silver slips. The subtle colors of the wood add a little warmth to the subdued coloring.

Where the edge of the paper or parchment is a feature, the map or document can be mounted onto a backing cardboard with another window mat on top to expose the edges. This practice is also frequently followed with prints, particularly etchings, where the paper, often handmade, is an essential element of the overall image.

Photographs
Old photographs usually look best in a frame of the same period, which is often similar to a watercolor frame, with a neutral-colored window mat and a thin molding. Intimate family photographs of past generations in soft sepia shades are often given fabric frames of velvet or leather.

▲ The narrow black-lacquered frame and minimal mat provide the perfect setting for this powerful print by Tsugumi Ota. A window mat has not been used, as the irregular edges of the paper form an integral part of the image. Frame by John Jones Frames.

▷ 148

▲ This strong woodblock print by Julian Meredith lent itself to a similar pattern on the frame, which is made of ash, scorched to deepen the grain, and then pickled (see page 74) for greater contrast. The frame is by Robert Cunning.

◀ An etching of children in the west of Ireland by Gerard Brockhurst has been framed in the traditional manner for prints, namely a thin black lacquer frame with a neutral off-white mat.

▲ A "Hogarth" style frame, made of oak with a gilt ball ornament on the sight edge, has been used for this decorative woodblock print of a pineapple. The warm colors of the print and the frame are offset by the cool blue of the mat. Both the etching and the frame are by Derek James.

▲ This lively watercolor by Rowlandson has a thin natural-wood frame that is lighter in color on the outer edge, with a thin line of gold on the sight edge. The double mat is decorated with pale wash lines on the inside, which complement the delicate shading in the picture.

These might be frames for a desk or table top, with a strut back, similarly covered in fabric.

Contemporary photographs, particularly "art photographs," are most often framed in an austere manner. Black and white photographs cannot usually stand much color on the frame, and thin black frames are widely used for modern displays of both color and black and white prints. This is a safe if unadventurous way to frame photographs. Natural wood, sometimes pickled, adds a restrained color which is suitable for the stark quality of many contemporary photographs.

At a recent exhibition of "master" photographers of the 1920s and 1930s at the Hayward Gallery in London, England, wide silver-gilt frames, distressed* to show a black clay undercoat, were used very effectively. This was a more dramatic style of framing, but the cool silver on black repeated the black and white of the photograph in a different key.

▲ This highly dramatic black-and-white photograph by Alex Ramsey needs a restrained presentation. The simple flat shape and restrained color of the pickled ash frame complement the image.

▶ An image like this photograph by Andy Goldsworthy, with its brilliant colors and wealth of detail, needs as little competition from the frame as possible. The plain, wide mat and narrow white square molding provide an elegant but unobtrusive setting. Frame by John Jones Frames.

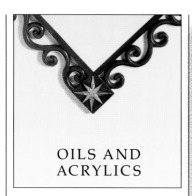

OILS AND ACRYLICS

Most oil and acrylic paintings are done on canvases (canvas stretched over a framework of wooden slats) or boards. Paintings on boards or panels present no problems for the framemaker, but canvases can become slightly distorted, and the overlap of canvas is thicker at the corners, so you will have to allow for these discrepancies, as well as making sure that the rabbet of the molding is deep enough to accommodate the wooden stretchers.

Oil and acrylics are more robust and less prone to damage than works on paper and thus do not usually need glass to protect them. Although most of the oil paintings you will see in many major art galleries do have glass, nowadays the majority are framed without it so that the texture of the paint surface is more readily appreciated. Mats are not used, and the moldings are usually wider than those traditionally used for works on paper.

There are exceptions to this rule. Small paintings done on thin board, with a fairly flat and unobtrusive paint surface, can benefit from being framed very much like watercolors, that is, glazed and mounted. A painting treated like this is

◀ The pale grays of the sky and water are an important feature in this painting by Peter Graham, and the frame has been painted to echo them, with a slightly warmer beige-gray on the inner slip frame. The width of the molding gives the frame an imposing presence, while the pale color prevents it from dominating the picture. Frame by Art Works, The Framemakers (Stephen Carruthers).

◀ The warm earth colors in this sunny landscape have been repeated in the terre verte (green) central border of burnished clay, and in the outer gilt edge which has been distressed to reveal the terracotta beneath. The frame and painting are by Ludmilla Thurlow.

▲ Very small paintings – this one is only about 8 in (20cm) across – often benefit from a wide, ornate frame. The painting is by David Warilow and the frame by John Jones Frames.

shown on page 154.

In general, small paintings look best in wide frames, which gives them additional presence, while large, bold paintings can often more or less stand by themselves, with a minimal frame or, in the case of pictures on canvas, a plain wood batten nailed around the edges. A floating frame*, in which the edges of the picture are not hidden by a rabbet, can look very effective, as this has the effect of thrusting the picture forward.

Apart from these general guidelines, there are no hard and fast rules, and over the centuries many different styles of frame have been used, ranging from the elaborate architectural motifs seen on frames of the Renaissance period, through carved, molded, and lavishly gilded frames to the more restrained natural wood or subtly decorated frames of the present time.

◀ At first sight, the frame seems very distinct from the picture, but there is a relationship, as the elaborate burnished black and silver frame has panels illustrating biblical stories. The central theme of the painting is the Flight to Egypt. The painting and frame are by Rosemary Williams.

▼ A floating frame allows the complete painting to be seen, as the edges are not covered by a rabbet. This painting by Adèle Seigal is on canvas, which stands proud of the dark gray inner frame. The frame was made by Harry Seigal.

✱FURTHER INFORMATION

Floating frames   page 49

OILS AND ACRYLICS

◀ Unusually, this painting has been given a cabinet-style frame with glass. The artist, George Rowlett, paints in thick impastos, building up almost three-dimensional effects, so this treatment is highly suitable both from an esthetic and a practical point of view – the peaks and crevices of thick paint collect dirt very quickly. Frame by John Jones Frames.

◀ This wide, gently curving reverse molding with no ornamentation sets off the painting very well. The starkness of the painted finish is relieved by a slight texture, and the inner slip provides a touch of warm color. The painting is by Peter Graham and the frame by Art Works, The Framemakers (Stephen Carruthers).

153

◄ Although the frame is older than the picture, which is a late Impressionist-style work, it combines well with this 19th-century molded frame. The pattern of the frame was softened with white color to subdue the gilt, little of which now remains.

► Again the Impressionist-style painting is displayed to advantage in a period frame. A few gilded highlights remain of the original gold pattern, which helps to lighten the frame color.

► Small oil paintings can look rather lost when hung on the wall. One solution is to use a wide, ornate frame, as in the example on page 151. Another is to treat them in a similar way to a watercolor, with a mat and glass. For works painted on thin cardboard, as this one is, the method is also practical, as the glass gives protection. The painting is by Jeremy Galton and the frame by Highgate Framers.

MIRROR FRAMES

Unlike other frames, those for mirrors have no competition – there is no picture to enhance, complement, or contrast with the frame. For this reason, the tradition of mirror frames is different to that of picture frames, owing more to the world of interior design. Some of the most inventive and beautiful mirror frames have been, and still are, made or designed by furniture makers. There are many historical examples of mirror frames, from the large carved pier glasses of the Rococo period to the more solid oak and mahogany hall mirrors of Victorian times.

Because the frames are made for their own sake, they can be as elaborate as you like in shape and design, with any paint finish or gilding effect you feel inclined to try out. If you are making a frame for a specific room, you will of course have to consider the existing decor, but otherwise there are no constraints.

One practical point to bear in mind is that a mirror will reflect the inside rabbet of the frame, so it must be painted (or gilded) in the same way as the rest of the frame. Otherwise, the natural color of the wood will show and detract from the overall effect.

▲ These highly ornate mirror frames with a carved and gilded imperial eagle on top were made in the Empire period in about 1820. The imperial taste was imported from France to England, and the frames were made in both countries at the beginning of the 19th century.

► A small vanity mirror frame has been made with imitation tortoiseshell (see page 124) laid onto a silver ground so that light is reflected through the shell. Black lacquer on each side gives a dramatic edge to the frame.

▼ The cassetta style, with a flat central section, lends itself to decoration, and here has been finely engraved (see page 126) with an arabic design. The gold has been distressed and colored for a mature appearance. Frame made by Aritotelis Zabetas.

▼ The extended corner (see page 42) featured here is a popular motif for mirror frames. The elaborate molded decoration around the frame has an Art Nouveau design on a "woven" background.

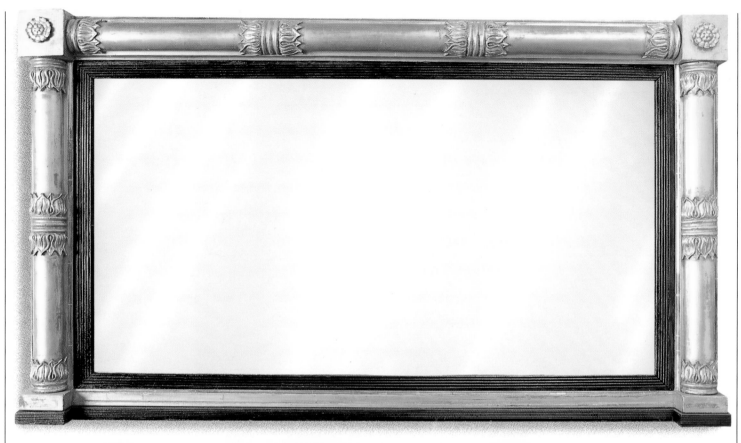

▲ The Neoclassical pillars at the side of this early 19th-century overmantel mirror are carried onto the top of the frame as well. The black reeded inner frame is repeated at the base of the frame.

◄ Antique picture frames are often used for mirrors, and this 19th-century molded frame with corner leaf and center ornaments is highly suitable.

► This square flat mirror frame has punched, painted, and sgraffito decorations (see pages 125 and 126) on a gold ground. The mirror has been made by laying silver leaf onto glass, giving an antique appearance. Frame and mirror by Rosemary Williams.

▼ A cassetta-style mirror frame with a sgraffito border of black over gold. The outer and sight edges are in bright burnished gold, and the mirror has been hand silvered. Frame and mirror made by Michele Riley.

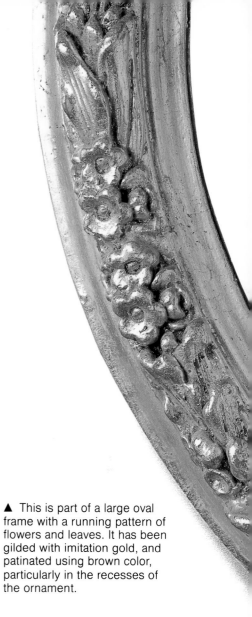

▲ This is part of a large oval frame with a running pattern of flowers and leaves. It has been gilded with imitation gold, and patinated using brown color, particularly in the recesses of the ornament.

TEXTILES AND OBJECTS

Textiles, whether woven or embroidered, have different physical characteristics from paintings, and some consideration needs to be given to this. Embroideries are sometimes framed without glass so that their texture can be seen and appreciated, but this does, of course, make them vulnerable to dirt and atmospheric conditions.

The majority of textiles, particularly valuable ones, are mounted and glazed to protect them. Frames can vary from thin, unobtrusive moldings to decorated ones using colors that complement or contrast those in the textile. The mounting of textiles can present a problem, as the conventional matte-surface colored matboard does not always make a suitable border. Fabric mats* can look effective, or double mats* with a gilded or contrast-colored inner border.

Textiles can also be framed without mats, treated rather like an oil painting, but with glass. This can be effective for bold, colorful embroideries or heavily textured ones such as needlepoint. It is important that the glass does not touch the embroidery, so a slip frame* or some form of insert is often used below the glass.

◄ These two crewel work embroideries based on Jacobean designs are intended to be hung as a pair and are framed almost identically, the only difference being in the mats. These are decorated with strands of the yarn used in the embroideries, oranges and yellows in one case and red in the other. Holes were pierced at the corners of the mat, and the yarn was pulled taut at the back, forming decorative textured lines of color. Embroideries and frames are by Barbara Skelt.

▶ This contemporary embroidery has been double-matted behind glass, and the blue color in the mat is repeated in the frame. The flat edge of the frame has been covered with veneer, and the central margin is gilded, a decorative style which complements this richly textured embroidery. The embroidery is by Bobby Britnell and the frame by Isabella Kocum.

▷ 162

Small objects – medals, jewelry, fans, feathers, and so on – and more three-dimensional type of embroidery such as stumpwork, where some of the shapes are padded – will need cabinet or box frames*. These not only provide sufficient depth to house the objects; they also enhance the presentation.

Most molding suppliers stock a variety of deep moldings for box frames, and standard molding profiles can be adapted by adding a further section of wood to the bottom. For simple displays, for example, a half- or quarter-round section can be added to the top of a section of wood 3 inches by 1 inch (7.5×2.5 cm) to make an effective deep frame. If glass is used, it must be held at the front of the frame, either using visible inner frames or invisible small blocks. The inside edges of the frame will be seen, so they must be taken into account in the overall decorative scheme.

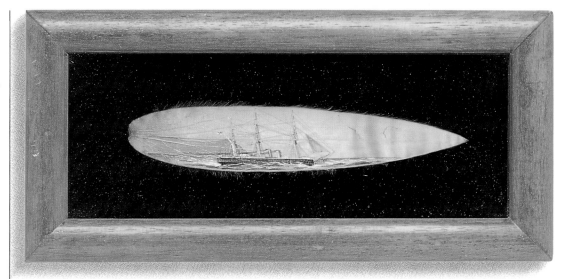

✱FURTHER INFORMATION

◄ This unusual object is a painting of a steamship on a leaf. It has been back-mounted onto black velvet and has a simple, natural-wood frame which traps the glass at the front as in a cabinet.

◄ This reverse appliqué design by Bobby Britnell has a repeating pattern which is echoed in the textured linear decoration of the frame. The pinks and purples in the textile have been picked up on the frame and highlighted with silver wax. The method used for texturing and painting the frame is shown on pages 84-85.

► This highly decorative embroidery with silver and gold stitching and elaborate floral margins needs a simple presentation. The natural wood frame has been pickled (see page 74), and the mat is a warm cream which sets off the rich coloring of the embroidery.

CLASSIC FRAMES

The development of picture framing is inextricably linked to that of architecture and furniture making, and when tastes in interior design changed and evolved, so did the design of frames. Paintings of earlier periods were often reframed in the prevailing taste of the time, and until quite recently in museums in Europe 15th- and 16th-century Italian paintings were often seen displayed in 18th- and 19th-century French and Northern European frames, reflecting the collector's taste rather than the period design. This was not considered odd or inappropriate, but recently more attention has been given to acquiring or reproducing the correct period frame for a particular picture. Along with this change has come a new appreciation of the artistry of the picture framer, and exhibitions of classic period frames are held.

Pre-Renaissance paintings were usually integral with their frames. The painting was done on the central part of a panel, which was cut out and planed so that a hollow area was formed. The surrounding bevel and ridge were often gilded and decorated. As paintings became more monumental, panels were joined together to form larger painted areas (canvas over stretchers was later used), and simple moldings were made to be attached to the panels.

Separate frames began to be made for the first time during the Renaissance, when tools and carpentry techniques became more sophisticated and the output of paintings increased dramatically. This was the great period of framemaking, and Renaissance designs still form the basis of many frames used today.

Italian design was copied and modified by the French and Spanish and the Northern European countries, and many distinctive styles evolved. The French made elaborately carved swept-shape frames, elegantly designed and richly gilded. Spanish frames were often darkly colored with heavily carved corner and center ornaments in gold. The Netherlands and the Protestant countries of Northern Europe tended toward a more austere style, with dark, heavy woods such as ebony and walnut carved in flutes and reeds with only small amounts of gold. These different cultures produced distinctive "classic" period frames which since the 19th century have been further copied and embellished. They are also often reproduced using molded rather than carved forms.

▲ These grand French Neoclassical frames of the 18th and 19th centuries have distinctive top ornaments, carved and modeled, with elaborate ribbons and wreaths. The top-heavy appearance is particularly suitable for mirrors and some portraits.

▶ A very lavish and richly carved frame surrounds this portrait of Queen Anne. The frame was made in England, and the dense and intricate carving is reminiscent of the great English woodcarver of the same period, Grinling Gibbons.

▲ These lovely Italian frames of the 17th and 18th centuries refer back to the designs and patterns of the Renaissance. They are richly decorated with sgraffito, engraved, and punched patterns and have borders of carved foliage.

UNUSUAL FRAMES

The most widely used shapes for frames, for obvious reasons, are rectangles and squares, though ovals and circles* are now becoming increasingly popular, as are hexagonal and octagonal frames*. The latter are no more difficult to make than rectangular frames, as most miter saws can be adjusted to the correct angle for the corners. Mat cutters* which will cut circles and ovals are now available, though the frames themselves are trickier to make.

Sometimes an image seems to call for a more unusual display, a famous example being the painting of a female nude by the Surrealist painter René Magritte, in which the wooden frame bends to follow the contours of the body. Another well-known Surrealist, Giorgio de Chirico, painted a triangular picture, which was naturally set in a triangular frame. Even when the image itself is a normal shape, an irregular-shaped frame can make an eye-catching wall display, and some craftsmen like to produce examples of unusual frames, particularly for mirrors, where there is no image to dictate the shape.

▲ This pedimented frame was made before the painting was done and suggested the classical theme of the picture. The whole frame has been marbled (see page 96), and the pillars have been marbled in a different color and gilded. The painting and frame are by Robert Cunning.

*FURTHER INFORMATION

Pentagons, hexagons, and
   octagons   page 50
Matcutters   page 16
Eggshell inlay   page 95

◀ John Anderson began by making frames for his own paintings, but gradually the frames actually became the paintings. He likes painting on wood or veneer and achieves background colors with alcohol-soluble dyes mixed with shellac, built up and burnished after each coat. For details, he uses acrylic, and he often includes touches of inlay, such as the bird in this example.

▲ The dramatic jagged and angular nature of the print has been carried through in an ingenious way onto the mat and frame. The frame is made with cutouts and appliqué wood sections. Frame and print are both by Ray Willingham.

▶ The flat border frame for this colorful pastel has been decorated by the artist, Frances Treanor, in a similar style and provides an intriguing extension of the painting.

▶ This unusual frame is decorated with eggshells and grouted so that it has the appearance of a mosaic. The oriental nature of the painting suggested this traditional Japanese technique, which is demonstrated on page 95. The painting and frame are by Derek James.

Triptych frames were initially conceived to transport elaborate altarpieces safely. The plain external doors protected the rich internal paintings and frames inside. Here, although there are also paintings on the outer doors, the idea has been retained by gilding the inner frame only. The doors have double rabbets to house the panels and are hinged on the outside of the central frame. The paintings and frame are by Robert Cunning.

▲ This "frame within a frame" has a small gilt inner surround attached to a backing card. The whole is glazed and contained within a traditional-style Dutch reeded frame. The painting is by Andrew Hewkin and the frame by James Frames (James Sullivan).

DISPLAYING PICTURES

There are no hard and fast rules about just where and how you should hang picture frames; the best rule of thumb is whether or not you like the finished results. However, there are guidelines you can follow regarding the grouping and arrangement.

Most pictures look best hung in groups to form a block rather than spaced out randomly over a large area. Unless a picture is fairly large, it is best not to hang it alone on the wall or it can look lost. The only exceptions are very large posters, prints, or ornate frames which are visually strong and imposing enough to make a statement by themselves.

Before you start to hammer picture nails in the wall, experiment with the layout by laying the framed images in groups on the floor. This will allow you to play around with sizes, shapes, and colors until you find a grouping you like. To work out the arrangement precisely, you can measure the wall space available and then mark out these boundaries on the floor with lengths of string.

Choosing the wall

Groups of pictures look best integrated as closely as possible with furnishings or any architectural features in a room. Use furniture as a guide for the outer vertical boundaries of your group. These might align with a sideboard or chest of drawers, for instance, in which case you can imagine a rectangle "drawn" on the wall up from the edges of the piece of furniture. This same principle works for the space above a bed or behind a couch.

The way your walls are decorated will dictate which pictures look best on them. White or plain light-colored walls look best with clear strong colors and pictures displayed in simple frames without mats. Monochrome prints and photos also look very effective on light walls. For colored walls, it is a good idea either to echo the color scheme of the room in the picture mat or to use the mat as an effective contrast. If walls are painted in dark solid colors, the pictures may need light-colored mats.

Patterned walls need the most care, as the picture and the wallcovering should not seem to be jostling with each other for attention. The coloring, size, and style of the wallcovering pattern will dictate the type of frame that looks best, but some sort of mat is almost always essential to give the picture clear definition.

Practicalities

While just about any flat vertical surface can become home to a picture frame, try not to hang pictures where they will be constantly knocked – in a narrow hall or close to the back of a chair – or you will be constantly having to straighten them.

▼ The narrow space between the windows is accentuated with a pair of matching prints in identical frames. Positioned above a side table, they draw the eye down toward the bowl of flowers and the table display.

Avoid hanging pictures above a radiator, as the rising heat, together with dust and grease carried upward, can damage the picture and may crack the glue of the frame. In general, pictures should not be hung in direct sunlight or opposite a window, especially if they are valuable. Watercolors are particularly vulnerable as they fade easily. In addition, if the picture is glazed, the reflection of the window can make it difficult to see the image.

Building a shape

If you have traditional picture rails, you can use picture hooks to support large frames hung on two chains – one at

each corner of the top of the frame. Repeat this idea around the room – the best effect comes from keeping the tops of all the pictures at the same height.

A group of pictures will look best if it does not appear to split obviously into either half or quarters. Groups that fall naturally into thirds tend to be more harmonious. Hang the central picture – the most eye-catching and interesting – at eye-level. This can either be your eye-level when standing or when seated; the latter could be effective in a dining room, for instance. As a rule, larger pictures look best when placed at the bottom of a group; otherwise, the arrangement can look top-heavy.

There are two basic types of grouping: geometric and informal. For the former, the pictures can be hung in a straight line or arranged in a neat square or rectangle. Formal geometric groups work best when the frame moldings are identical and the pictures the same shape and size. This style works well with modern furnishings and is a good way to display a set of matching prints or photographs.

A geometric picture arrangement can be used either to emphasize or to play down the proportions of a room. A long horizontal line of pictures will have the effect of lessening the height of a tall, lofty ceiling, while a tall column of pictures takes the eye up and makes a room with a low ceiling seem taller and more spacious.

For pictures of different sizes, shapes, and types, you will need an informal arrangement. Be prepared to experiment to find the most pleasing distribution of shapes – it may help to imagine the outline of the group forming a rectangle, circle, or triangle. Generally, large pictures look best with fairly wide gaps between them, while smaller pictures need to be hung closer together to avoid a sparse appearance.

Lighting

Not all pictures look best when strongly lit. You may wish to highlight the central frame in a group or highlight just one or two smaller frames. Apart from natural daylight, there are basically two ways to light pictures: either by spotlighting (positioning an ordinary light or spotlight to shine onto the picture from somewhere in the room) or by fixing a light on or near the frame itself. Experiment using the types of lamp mentioned below until you find exactly the effect you want.

Uplights give an even, diffused light. They can be positioned on a table, on the floor directly under the frames, or hidden among foliage or behind a chair. Spotlights can be adjusted to create direct or reflected light. Low-voltage tungsten-halogen spotlights are small and discreet, and can be used as ceiling lights, as individual wall-spots, or in a standard-style floor fitting; two or more individual spots can be mounted on a strip track attached to the wall or ceiling.

A fluorescent strip will light a complete group of pictures. A good technique to use in a large room is to fit a diffuser to angle the light onto the pictures and choose a "daylight" colored bulb for the most natural effect.

Picture lights are individual units attached directly to the picture or to the wall just above it. They are available in a range of modern and traditional styles, so can be chosen to match both your room and the picture. Make sure the fitting is wide enough to light the whole picture – it should be about two-thirds of the picture's width. If it throws a reflection on the glass or varnish, you can reduce it simply by tilting the picture slightly toward the floor.

▲ An eclectic mixture of frames in different sizes, shapes, and with very different images fills one complete wall. Careful positioning of frames keeps the balance correct between large and small-sized frames. With a plain dark background of cork tiles, each picture needs either a contrasting frame or a colored mat to help it stand out. The single picture on the right is large enough – and with a strong image – to make a statement all on its own.

GLOSSARY

Aniline dyes
Synthetic dyes originally made from aniline, a colorless, oily liquid. The dyes are bought in powdered form and can be mixed with denatured alcohol to make wood dyes, or with **Shellac** to make colored lacquers and varnishes.

Beading
Narrow strip of wood, often ornamental, sometimes used as an additional component of a frame.

Beeswax
Natural wax made from honeycombs, used on its own as a polish or as a base for colored polishes and imitation golds (*see* **Bronze powders**).

Bevel
The sloping edge on the inside window of a **Mat**; the sloping edge of a ruler used for cutting bevels.

Biscuit joiner
A miniature saw that cuts grooves across the backs of miter joints into which a wedge of wood is inserted to strengthen them.

Bole *see* **Burnishing clay**

Box frames
Deep frames designed to display three-dimensional objects such as medals behind glass. Also used for embroideries and sometimes for oil paintings with a particularly thick build-up of paint. Sometimes called cabinet frames.

Bronze powder
Finely powdered base metals, usually bronze, used to make imitation gold and gold paint.

Burnishers
Tools used in the water-gilding method to rub the gold or silver leaf to a smooth, shiny finish. Traditional burnishers have smooth, curved ends made of agate, set in plain wooden handles.

Burnishing clay
Fine clay colored with pigment, used in the preparation of surfaces for gilding. The traditional color used under gold leaf is dark terracotta, but the clay is available in a number of different colors. It can be bought as a paste or in a solid cone.

Button polish *see under* **Shellac**

Cabinet frames *see* **Box frames**

Carnauba wax
Wax obtained from the leaves of the Brazilian fan-palm tree, used with beeswax in the preparation of gold and silver waxes.

Carragheen moss
Type of seaweed used in combination with special inks for marbling paper.

Casein
Strongly adhesive substance made from the curd of milk. Used as a binder for paint and as a glue. A form of **Gesso** can be made using casein as an alternative to **Rabbit-skin glue**.

Cassetta frame
A traditional type of frame which has a border within an outer molding. The borders are often richly decorated.

Conservation board
Matboard made from rag or woodpulp specially treated to remove acids, which can be harmful to valuable works on paper.

Craquelure
The fine cracks often seen on old oil paintings. The effect is sometimes deliberately induced on frames by putting a fast-drying paint or varnish over a slow-drying one.

Decoupage
Form of decoration in which pieces of cut paper are glued to the frame molding and then treated with successive layers of varnish. The paper used can be plain colored paper, photographic or other images from magazines, or photostats, either colored or black and white.

Distressing
Method of simulating the patina of age on a frame by rubbing away some of the top layer of gilt or paint so that the base color shows through.

Epoxy resins
Chemically synthesized resin glues, usually in two parts, the glue itself and a hardener. Some epoxy resins are bought in powder form, with the hardener incorporated, and are mixed with water.

Floating frame
A frame designed so that the picture does not fit behind a rabbet, but either stands proud of its border or is flush with it. Floating frames are mainly used for oil or acrylic paintings on panels, where the image extends fully to the edges.

Foxing
The brown spots of mildew often seen on old mats, prints, or watercolors, caused by damp.

French polish *see under* **Shellac**

Fuming
Coloring wood by exposing it to the fumes of ammonia.

Gesso
Brilliant white preparation made from whiting (chalk) and **Rabbit-skin glue** size or **Casein** size, used to prepare surfaces for gilding before the application of **Burnishing clay**. Acrylic gesso, bought ready made, is produced principally as a ground for paintings and is less suitable for preparing wood surfaces, as it cannot be sanded to such a smooth surface.

Gilt
The term covering all water-gilded or transfer-gilded surfaces, whether gold or silver. *See also* **Gold leaf, Transfer gilding, Water gilding**.

Glazing
The word has two meanings. 1: to cover a picture with glass; 2: to apply a thin, transparent layer of color over another color.

Glazing gun
A type of stapler which shoots flat, triangular-shape tacks into the back of the frame to secure the glass.

Gold leaf
Thin sheets of beaten gold (or silver) applied over a surface prepared with **Gesso** and **Burnishing clay**. The leaf used in **Transfer gilding** has a paper backing.

Gold size
A viscous glue substance traditionally used in **Transfer gilding** to secure the gold or silver leaf to the prepared surface. A water-soluble glue has now been developed as an alternative.

Graining
Simulating the grain of wood with paints and glazes applied over an undercoat. Inexpensive wood can be treated in this way to resemble a rare and exotic one.

Hide glue
Animal-skin glue obtained as granules which are mixed with water and heated before use. This was the traditional glue for

woodworking before the advent of the various synthetic glues.

Lacquer
A hard, glossy paint made with cellulose derivatives or by dissolving pigments or aniline dyes in **Shellac**.

Mat
The card surround used to protect and display a work on paper. Mats are usually cut with a window behind which the picture fits, and the inner edges are beveled.

Miter
The 45° angled cut made in each end of a piece of frame molding so that they meet at a 90° angle (miter joint).

Miter saw
A saw designed specifically for cutting miters. The blade is held in place by two steel columns mounted on a metal base.

Molding
A shaped length of wood. Picture-frame moldings have a **Rabbet** behind which the picture fits (and the mat and glass if used). Carpenter's moldings, used for baseboards, trimmings around doors, etc., have no rabbet, but can sometimes be adapted for framemaking.

Pastiglia
An extra-thick **Gesso** used for ornamental work on frames. Patterns are built up in relief and then gilded.

Pickling
Treating raw wood by pushing white pigment into the grain. Oak and ash are the woods most commonly pickled.

Polyurethane varnish
Frequently used instead of French polish (see under **Shellac**) to finish and protect natural wood. It is available in gloss and flat finishes, and is tough and durable. However, it tends to discolor with time.

Profile
The word used to describe the shape of a **Molding**.

Ox gall
A medium used in the manufacture of watercolors and also sometimes as a paint medium. It breaks the tension of the water and makes the paint flow more freely.

Rabbet
The L-shaped groove on the inside edge of a picture-frame molding into which the picture, glass, mat, and backing board fit. Sometimes called rebate.

Rabbit-skin glue
Bought in granules and mixed and heated to make glue or size. It is used for treating raw wood to make it less absorbent, and in the preparation of **Gesso**. (See also **Casein**.)

Rag rolling
Method of decorating wood by laying down paint and pushing a rag in various directions along it to produce a textured effect.

Reverse molding
A molding which has the highest part next to the picture and slopes away at the outer edge.

Router
A machine used by professional framemakers for cutting molding shapes, grooves, and rabbets.

Sgraffito
A method of decoration in which fine lines and patterns are scratched into a top layer of paint or gilt, leaving the color beneath showing through.

Shellac
A varnish made from a resin secreted by the lac insect, suspended in alcohol. It is variously colored from pale yellow to dark brown, and is known by a number of different names, including French polish, button polish, and garnet polish. It can also be mixed with **Aniline dyes**. Shellac seals the grain and

protects the wood, but is neither heat- nor spirit-resistant.

Sight edge
The inner edge of the frame molding, next to the picture.

Size
A weak solution of glue used to seal wood and reduce its absorbency before painting, and as an ingredient in the preparation of **Gesso**. (See also **Casein** and **Rabbit-skin glue**.)

Slip frame
A flat, narrow strip of wood, sometimes gilded or decorated, inserted between the main frame and the picture. Slips are often used to protect the picture by providing more space between it and the glass, but they can also be purely decorative.

Spattering
Decorating a surface by flicking droplets of paint over it. Spattering can achieve subtle and complex effects of color, and can be used for both frames and mats.

Sponging
Creating textured effects by applying paint with a sponge, or laying a coat of paint and then dabbing into it. This method can also be used for both frames and mats.

Tabernacle frame
A traditional type of frame which has a decorative panel or pediment fitted to the top. Now used more frequently for mirrors than for pictures.

Three-dimensional frame see **Box frame**.

Transfer gilding
Method of gilding in which glue is used to fasten the gold leaf to the prepared surface. The leaf usually has a paper backing, which is peeled off once the gilt is in place. The process is faster and easier than **Water gilding**, but transfer leaf cannot be burnished.

Trimmer
A tool used for trimming the end-grain of wood, for both **Miters** and 90° cuts.

Underpinner
A machine used by professional framemakers to join the frame by shooting metal wedges into the back of the miter joint. Hand-operated underpinners are now becoming available.

Veneer
Thin sheets of wood which can be bonded to the surface of a less expensive wood. Some of the rarer and more exotic woods are only available as veneers.

Wash line
A form of decoration used on mats, usually for watercolors or old prints. A pale wash of watercolor is painted around the whole mat a small distance from the window, and finished with fine pen lines.

Water gilding
The traditional method of gilding, in which loose gold or silver leaf is applied to a surface prepared with **Gesso** and **Burnishing** clay. No glue is used.

White glue
Polyvinyl acetate, a synthetic resin glue in the form of a thick white liquid. Now the glue most commonly used in framemaking and other woodworking. In a diluted form, white glue can also be used as a paint medium.

Whiting
A fine chalk which, together with **Rabbit-skin glue size**, is the principal ingredient of **Gesso**. The best is called gilder's whiting.

INDEX

Page numbers in *italic* refer to the illustrations

CREDITS

The author and publishers would like to thank all those who made their frames available for photography. Wherever possible, the makers of frames are credited in the captions to the illustrations, but we would also like to thank those who kindly loaned frames, equipment or photographs, but whose names do not appear in the book. **Mary Alliston LMPA,** page 73; **Faber Blinds** pages 170, 171; **J. Fisher and Son,** page 18; **Franchis Locks and Tools,** pages 14-15; **Bryant Jackson Communications (Arquati mouldings),** pages 21, 119; **Lapis,** page 151; **Cathy Meeus,** pages 142, 146 bottom, 147, 145 top, 155; **Paul Mitchell Antiques Ltd,** pages 164-5; **Now and Then,** pages 148-9, 156-7; **Origin Framing Supplies,** pages 13, 16-17, 21, 58, 77; **Paperchase,** pages 61, 62; **Porter Design,** page 140; **Dr and Mrs Wynne Williams,** page 162 top.

The author offers particular thanks to the following for their invaluable help in the preparation of this book. **Isabella Kocum** for gilding and decorating frames; **John Spencer** for making and decorating mounts; **Louise Taylor** for her demonstration of wood graining; **Derek James, Martin Britnell** and **Alistair MacDonald** for making frames, and **Jana Valencic** for general organization and administration.

749
CUN

Cunning, Robert

The encyclopedia of
picture framing
techniques

$24.95

DATE